T0323617

Cambridge Elements ≡

Elements in Politics and Society in East Asia
edited by
Erin Aeran Chung
The Johns Hopkins University
Mary Alice Haddad
Wesleyan University
Benjamin L. Read
University of California, Santa Cruz

THE ADAPTABILITY OF THE CHINESE COMMUNIST PARTY

Martin K. Dimitrov
Tulane University

CAMBRIDGE
UNIVERSITY PRESS

Shaftesbury Road, Cambridge CB2 8EA, United Kingdom

One Liberty Plaza, 20th Floor, New York, NY 10006, USA

477 Williamstown Road, Port Melbourne, VIC 3207, Australia

314–321, 3rd Floor, Plot 3, Splendor Forum, Jasola District Centre,
New Delhi – 110025, India

103 Penang Road, #05–06/07, Visioncrest Commercial, Singapore 238467

Cambridge University Press is part of Cambridge University Press & Assessment,
a department of the University of Cambridge.

We share the University's mission to contribute to society through the pursuit of
education, learning and research at the highest international levels of excellence.

www.cambridge.org
Information on this title: www.cambridge.org/9781009517126

DOI: 10.1017/9781009184335

First published 2024

A catalogue record for this publication is available from the British Library

ISBN 978-1-009-51712-6 Hardback
ISBN 978-1-009-18443-4 Paperback
ISSN 2632-7368 (online)
ISSN 2632-735X (print)

The Adaptability of the Chinese Communist Party

Elements in Politics and Society in East Asia

DOI: 10.1017/9781009184335
First published online: December 2024

Martin K. Dimitrov
Tulane University

Author for correspondence: Martin K. Dimitrov, mdimitro@tulane.edu

Abstract: The Chinese Communist Party (CCP) celebrated its 100th birthday in 2021. Its durability poses a twofold question: How has the party survived thus far? And is its survival formula sustainable in the future? This Element argues that the CCP has displayed a continuous capacity for adaptation, most recently in response to the 1989 Tiananmen protests and the collapse of communism in Europe. As the CCP evaluated the lessons of 1989, it identified four threats to single-party rule: economic stagnation; socioeconomic discontent; ideological subversion; and political pluralism. These threats have led to adaptive responses: allowing more private activity; expansion of the social safety net; promotion of indigenous cultural production; and rival incorporation into the party. Although these responses have enabled the CCP to survive thus far, each is reaching its limit. As adaptation stagnates, the strategy has been to increase repression, which creates doubt about the ongoing viability of single-party rule.

Keywords: Chinese Communist Party, cultural security, rival incorporation, economic reform, welfare expansion

ISBNs: 9781009517126 (HB), 9781009184434 (PB), 9781009184335 (OC)
ISSNs: 2632-7368 (online), 2632-735X (print)

Contents

1 Introduction: The Adaptability of the Chinese Communist Party   1

2 Economic Reform   12

3 Extending the Social Safety Net   21

4 Protecting Cultural Security and Promoting Indigenous Cultural Consumption   33

5 Rival Incorporation into the Chinese Communist Party   47

6 Conclusion   65

Abbreviations   71

References   72

1 Introduction: The Adaptability of the Chinese Communist Party

In 2021 the Chinese Communist Party (CCP) celebrated its 100th birthday (Saich 2021; Dickson 2021; Shambaugh 2021; Cheek, Mühlhahn, and van de Ven 2021). Other communist parties have also reached this milestone – but only after the single-party system they had established and overseen had been definitively dissolved. Unique about the CCP is that it turned 100 when it was still in power. From this point of view, the more significant achievement of 2021 is that the CCP marked seventy-two years as a ruling party. As of 2024, it has reached its seventy-fifth anniversary governing the People's Republic of China (PRC). Its durability poses a twofold question: How has the party been able to survive thus far? And will its survival formula be sustainable in the future?

This Element argues that the CCP has displayed a continuous capacity for adaptation (Heilmann and Perry 2011), most recently in response to the 1989 Tiananmen protests and the collapse of communism in Europe (Shambaugh 2008; Dimitrov 2013). As the CCP evaluated the lessons of 1989, it identified four threats to single-party rule: economic stagnation; socioeconomic discontent; ideological subversion; and political pluralism. These threats have led to adaptive responses: allowing more private activity; expansion of the social safety net; promotion of indigenous cultural production; and incorporation of rivals into the party. These adaptations have enabled the CCP to survive thus far, yet each is reaching its limit. As these adaptive responses have stagnated, the dominant strategy has been to increase repression, which in turn is creating doubt about the long-term viability of the current single-party model.

1.1 The Durability of the CCP in Comparative Context

Although democratization made significant advances around the globe in the twentieth century, progress in the last two decades has stalled. Currently, four-fifths of the world's population lives in nondemocratic polities (Freedom House 2024, 10). Democracy promoters have come to realize that authoritarianism is an enduring phenomenon that cannot be vanquished by triumphalist thinking about the end of history (Fukuyama 1989). Therefore, an understanding of the sources of autocratic longevity is an urgent initial step for those who seek to develop strategies for democratic consolidation in the twenty-first century.

Comparative research demonstrates that there is significant variation in the lifespans of autocracies (Magaloni 2006; Brownlee 2007). A tripartite division of nondemocracies (no parties; multiple parties; single party) indicates that single-party regimes exhibit the highest longevity (Svolik 2012, 186). Within the group of single-party regimes, communist dictatorships have outlasted noncommunist

Table 1 Average tenure of autocracies, 1946–2008

Regime type	N	Tenure (years)
Parties banned	81	16.6
Multiple parties	195	15.9
Noncommunist single-party	51	29.9
Collapsed communist single-party (1991)	10	48.3
Surviving communist single-party (2024)	5	67

Sources: Smith 2005; Svolik 2012, esp. 184–192; author's calculations.

autocracies, emerging as the most resilient type of nondemocratic system. There are notable differences in the durability of two different subsets of communist regimes (see Table 1). As is well known, most communist systems collapsed in 1989–91. Yet, China, North Korea, Vietnam, Laos, and Cuba have persisted for more than three decades since the end of the Cold War. As of 2024, the average tenure of these five single-party regimes is sixty-seven years. This is an extraordinary record of durability. China stands out even within this group of durable regimes. In 2023, it matched the longevity of the Communist Party of the Soviet Union, which ruled for seventy-four years. Only the Korean Workers Party has governed longer than the CCP, celebrating its seventy-fifth year in power in 2023.

Some might wonder whether China can still be usefully described as a communist state. The classic typology developed by scholars of dictatorships might be relevant to address this question (Friedrich and Brzezinski 1965, 22). Organizationally, the CCP today appears little different from the party that has ruled the country during the previous seven decades. There is no political pluralism and opposition parties are still proscribed. Central planning no longer exists, but the party exercises both direct and indirect control over economic activity. The CCP maintains a monopoly over the use of force and directs repression against regime enemies. Although Marxism–Leninism is no longer the dominant ideology, the regime is committed to preventing harmful ideological influences from entering the country. The means of mass communication remain under the control of the party-state. In sum, though some scholars may see communist states as an anachronism, China today is a recognizable yet upgraded exemplar of this regime type.

Had China simply survived as a single-party state, its record of longevity past the watershed year of 1989 would have still required an explanation. Yet, it has thrived economically and has managed to contain discontent and calls for political liberalization. To understand this exceptional resilience, we need to identify the adaptive responses that have made it possible.

1.2 The Adaptive Capacity of the CCP

Scholarly understandings of the adaptive capacity of the CCP reflect the evolution of the discipline of political science. Until the Eastern European and Soviet collapses, the general consensus was that communist regimes will persist (Kuran 1991), regardless of whether scholars conceptualized them as totalitarian polities incapable of evolution (Friedrich and Brzezinski 1965) or acknowledged the possibility of dynamic change (Bunce 1981; Oi 1985; Hauslohner 1987). In a sharp reversal, following the Soviet collapse, political scientists began to doubt the staying power of the remaining communist regimes, including that in China. Scholars anticipated a coming collapse (Chang 2001), variously attributed to rising prosperity (Rowen 1996), disaffected elites (Gilley 2004), or socioeconomic pressures fueled by extreme corruption stemming from the lack of political reform (Pei 2006). The tenor of these arguments maintained that ossification prevented dynamic change. However, simultaneous with such pessimistic accounts of China's future, two novel propositions have emerged. One stresses the resilience of the system, focusing on the increasingly predictable and meritocratic nature of elite politics, on the more clearly specified mandates of institutions, and on opportunities for citizen participation (Nathan 2003). Another proposition emphasizes the atrophy of the CCP after the Soviet collapse but it also suggests that there have been signs of adaptation, especially in the realm of inner-party democracy and ideological acceptance of capitalists (Shambaugh 2008). The field of China studies thus entered the 2010s with the two images of resilience and adaptation. In contrast to the 1990s, the consensus in the 2010s was that China was not threatened by imminent collapse.

The 2010s and early 2020s have been marked by a search to identify the reasons for the resilience of the Chinese political system (Hsu, Tsai, and Chang 2021). Considering the complexity of the issue, there are variations in the following explanations. Some scholars point to repression and social control (Mattingly 2020; Ong 2022; Byler 2022), as well as to the co-optation of religious organizations (Reny 2018). Others develop arguments about the regime-sustaining effects of economic growth (Ang 2020). Those studying elite politics stress the skillful management of factional conflict and rivalries (Fewsmith 2021; Shih 2022). Popular support for the party and its domestic and foreign policies is highlighted as well (Dickson 2016; 2021; Shirk 2007; 2023; Weiss 2014). With regard to adaptation, some scholars emphasize the repurposing or retrofitting of institutions (Oi and Goldstein 2018; Gueorguiev 2021), whereas others focus on experimentation in governance techniques, what they call a "guerrilla policy style" (Heilmann and Perry 2011).

How does the present Element relate to existing studies of adaptation and resilience? According to Heilmann and Perry, resilience is "the capacity of a system to experience and absorb shocks and disturbances," whereas adaptability is "the capacity of actors in a system to further resilience" (Heilmann and Perry 2011, 8). I adopt a different view, conceptualizing resilience as the long-term outcome of adaptive change (Dimitrov 2013, 7). Adaptive change refers to a complex causal process that involves experiencing a shock and then implementing changes in light of the lessons learned from that shock. The approach of this Element bears similarities to those of Shambaugh (2008) and Dickson (2016) who respectively describe the doctrinal adjustments and practical steps that have allowed the promotion of private entrepreneurial activity as a type of adaptive change implemented by the CCP during reform and opening following the shock of Mao's ill-considered economic policies. Before we proceed further, we should stress that this Element does not seek to provide a historical treatment of the evolution of the CCP (Saich 2021) or of the complex ways in which the CCP manages Chinese society (Dickson 2021). Its goals are squarely focused on the adaptive responses the CCP has deployed since 1989 to avert the collapse of the single-party model of rule in China.

Building on existing studies that highlight individual adaptations, this Element offers a unified framework for understanding earlier arguments by highlighting the specific adaptations undertaken in response to 1989. "Adaptation" is often used loosely in the literature. The Merriam-Webster definition is "modification of an organism or its parts that makes it more fit for existence under the conditions of its environment." The definition that this Element adopts encompasses the policy changes instituted by the CCP in light of the lessons learned from the shock of 1989, which produced the fundamental insight that communist regimes cannot avoid collapse without proactive measures. The focus here is the specific effects of 1989. At the same time, the approach is broad because it reveals that the scale of the shock necessitated learning general lessons which subsequently led to a set of wide-ranging adaptations (of the economy, of welfare provision, of the ideological sphere, and of party building) that may appear unconnected unless one looks at them through the unified prism of the CCP's reactions to the momentous events of 1989. The unanticipated near-collapse of communism in China and its surprising demise in two-thirds of the countries constituting the communist universe necessitated introducing comprehensive measures aimed at ensuring the continued dominance of the CCP. Our discussion of these adaptive policy responses forms the core of this Element.

1.3 Learning from 1989

The CCP has implemented adaptive changes in response to shocks at various points in China's political development. Apart from 1989, there have been other turbulent times in China's political history that have led to adaptations. A major contender for that status is 1976, when Chairman Mao died. How do 1976 and 1989 differ? Unquestionably, the death of China's founding leader was a significant event. Nevertheless, while unprecedented in the Chinese context, such a crisis also occurred in various other communist regimes prior to 1976 and was, invariably, successfully resolved. The Chinese leadership operated with full knowledge of these historical precedents. Although other types of autocracies may be unable to survive the death of a founding leader (Meng 2020), there is no evidence that this has ever occurred in the communist universe. In China, as in the Soviet Union after the death of Stalin, the demise of Mao led to elite reshuffling and opened an opportunity for adopting a softer governance model. By contrast, 1989 presented a crisis that was potentially insurmountable. At stake was not only who China's next leader would be but also the viability of the entire political system. The domestic and international events of 1989 presented an existential threat to the CCP and its single-party model. Surviving the shock of 1989 required substantially more wide-ranging adaptations than the relatively less threatening death of the founding leader in 1976. Other shocks have been experienced in the decades since 1989 as well: Falun Gong in 1999; the democracy and minority rights movements in 2008; and the Severe Acute Respiratory Syndrome (SARS) and COVID-19 public health crises in 2003 and 2020–22. However, these shocks pale in comparison to the existential challenge presented by the events of 1989.

In 1989, the CCP experienced a dual shock. The initial component was domestic, as China was rocked by protests that directly challenged the top party leadership and called for political liberalization along the lines of *glasnost* in the Soviet Union. There was also urban worker discontent, which stemmed from high inflation and from plans to proceed with marketization by dismantling lifetime state employment and the accompanying cradle-to-grave benefits known as the "iron rice bowl" (*tie fanwan*). The party weathered the nationwide protests of April–June 1989 successfully. Yet, there was a second shock which was more protracted and whose impact on the party was less straightforward. That second process began on June 4, 1989, the day when the leadership, with the help of tanks, cleared Tiananmen Square of all protesters. Ironically, June 4, 1989, was also the day when Solidarity won a surprising victory in the first round of elections in communist Poland. That win set in motion the collapse of other communist regimes and concluded with the dissolution of the Soviet Union on Christmas

Day 1991. In this Element, references to the international aspects of "1989" encompass the entire 1989–91 period which saw the collapse of ten communist regimes (Albania, Bulgaria, Czechoslovakia, the German Democratic Republic, Hungary, Mongolia, Poland, Romania, the Soviet Union, and Yugoslavia). Those international events placed in context what had occurred domestically in China in 1989, revealing that the entire system was in danger. As communist regimes were disappearing around the world (due to political and socioeconomic contention combined with leadership divisions and minority unrest in ethnically heterogeneous regimes), there was growing uncertainty among Chinese leaders about the long-term viability of the single-party model. This necessitated lesson-learning and subsequent implementation of relevant adaptive changes.

We should define what constitutes "learning." In the behavioral and brain sciences, learning refers to the acquisition of behavior that allows an animal to solve a particular problem (like feeding) that results from a change in the environment (Johnston 1981). The parallel with China is clear: 1989 produced a catastrophic change in the environment (both domestic and international events demonstrated that communist regimes were more fragile than previously thought) that presented the problem of how to develop behavior that would allow the CCP to ensure its survival. The adaptations reviewed in this Element were implemented with the conscious goal of avoiding regime collapse. The process of learning has been iterative, with ongoing attention by China's top leaders to any threats to communist rule, as revealed by the paradigmatic case of 1989. A counterfactual might be useful here: had 1989 not occurred, the leadership would not have been compelled to engage in the recursive in-depth discussions that generated dynamic lessons leading to the specific adaptations discussed throughout this Element. We may want to recall that Francis Fukuyama, writing immediately before Tiananmen, saw China as the place where history would end due to the inevitable pressures for political reform generated by the flourishing of economic liberalism (Fukuyama 1989, esp. 11–12). Without 1989 and without learning from what occurred, China might not be a communist regime today.

1.4 Evidence of Learning: Internal Chinese Assessments of the Soviet Collapse

Authoritarian regimes are characterized by a culture of secrecy. This presents a methodological problem for those studying China: How can we identify with a reasonable degree of certainty how the CCP views a certain issue? Two options exist. The first is to rely on what has been called "public artefacts" (Barros 2016), such as easily accessible speeches, official government documents, and reports in the state media. Although important research has been done using such materials, analysts must be mindful when interpreting public artefacts that they are equivocal sources. Especially relevant within a culture of secrecy is the fact that the party has decided to make these documents publicly accessible, thus raising questions about why they have been allowed to circulate. As scholars cannot easily get clear answers to such questions, interpreting public artefacts is not straightforward. A second option for studying polities characterized by opacity is to rely on government documents not meant for public dissemination. In China, these sources are generally known as *neibu* (for internal circulation), although there can be various levels of classification that exceed *neibu*, such as *jimi* (secret) and *juemi* (top secret). Scholars have used such leaked government documents to study issues like the 1989 Tiananmen protests (Zhang 2001), the Xinjiang camps (Uyghur Tribunal 2021), and propaganda (King, Pan, and Roberts 2017; Pan and Chen 2018). Typically, *neibu* materials can be found in repositories in China, Hong Kong, Taiwan, the United States, and Europe. Because the documents are generated with no expectation that they will fall into outsiders' hands, *neibu* sources have the potential to reveal what regime insiders think (Dimitrov 2023). This Element makes use of such materials.

These materials show that Deng Xiaoping and his successors Jiang Zemin, Hu Jintao, and Xi Jinping have all been deeply concerned about the importance of the CCP learning from the demise of the Soviet Union (Dimitrov 2019). Dozens of leadership speeches have been delivered and thousands of academic articles and books have been published on the lessons of the Soviet collapse (Guan 2010). There have even been several high-profile *neibu* documentaries that were screened to party cadres, highlighting the lessons that top leaders wanted them to draw from the Soviet dissolution. Although more than three decades have elapsed since this event, it remains important to the present. Studying the Soviet collapse and learning from it is not an arcane academic question. Rather, it is of existential importance to the CCP.

The paramount lesson focuses on the imperative of preserving the CCP monopoly on power, with the corollary that political liberalization is not to be allowed. Specifically, the voluminous analyses can be reduced to two additional overarching conclusions. The first concerns the economy: ongoing gradual marketization with attention to the losers from the reforms is necessary. This stands in contrast to the big-bang approach to dismantling the state socialist economies, which is accompanied by extraordinary social costs. The second lesson comprises the importance of maintaining ideological vigilance against hostile foreign forces (*didui shili*) bent on subverting the single-party system through a strategy of peaceful evolution (*heping yanbian*) (Zuo 2022). In combination with repression, these strategies (focusing on party building, economic reform, welfare provision, and cultural security) have ensured the stability of single-party rule in China. The implementation of such strategies requires ongoing adaptations, which are discussed in the remainder of this section.

1.5 Specific Adaptations Implemented after 1989

The CCP deployed four adaptative responses, consistent with the major conclusions it had reached by analyzing the events of 1989. The first adaptation stems from the understanding that the scope of the inefficient centrally planned economy had to be reduced in favor of allowing more space for the market. We should keep in mind that there was significant opposition to reform, fueled in part by negative attitudes toward the former Soviet Union and several Eastern European states that had adopted a program of radical economic restructuring, known as the "Harvard Plan," as its key architects Jeffrey Sachs and Andrei Shleifer were based at the Harvard Institute for International Development. After prolonged deliberation, the party had to proceed with economic reform carefully but firmly. Within two decades, the private sector became China's dominant employer and contributed more than half of the nation's gross domestic product (GDP). Yet, this process of expansion faced clear redlines: entrepreneurs could not have full economic autonomy; could not use their riches to obtain political power; and could not operate without creating party cells. The party maintained and bolstered state-owned enterprises (SOEs) in strategic industries even after China's World Trade Organization (WTO) entry, as we discuss in Section 2. The private sector has not been allowed to challenge the primacy of the CCP. This stands in marked contrast to the experience of post-Soviet Russia, where the oligarchs literally moved into the Kremlin under Yeltsin and "captured the state" (Freeland 2000; Klebnikov 2000; Hoffman 2002).

A related second adaptation involves protecting the reform losers by extending the social safety net (Duckett 2011; Cook and Dimitrov 2017; Huang 2020). One reason for the Tiananmen unrest was the uncertainty among workers regarding how they might be affected by the bankruptcies of urban enterprises that would inevitably accompany the transition from plan to market (Walder and Gong 1991). To soften the impact of job losses and the dismantling of preexisting welfare benefits, the party delayed reform of the inefficient urban industrial enterprises until the second half of the 1990s. Urban workers were allowed to purchase, at submarket rates, their enterprise-supplied housing and were given a generous period of time to be retrained for new positions. In the 2000s and 2010s, benefits like healthcare and pensions, which under Mao had been reserved primarily for urban workers, came to be extended nearly universally. This major expansion was driven by the necessity of maintaining stability, which emerged from the domestic shock of 1989 and from analyses of the experience of the transitional economies of Eastern Europe, where the dismantling of the extremely generous socialist welfare state, along with widespread unemployment and hyperinflation, cultivated significant levels of opposition to the market economy and led to the voting out of office of those political elites who were promoting it. The CCP did not want to find itself left in a similar position.

The third adaptation stems from the understanding that the events of 1989, both domestically and in the Eastern Bloc, reflected the impact of external ideological subversion (Guojia Anquan Bu 1990b; Guojia Anquan Bu 1991). Foreign cultural products were seen as conduits for the promotion of Western values that presented a direct threat to the party-state. Instead of relying solely on censorship of foreign media, the CCP also promoted the consumption of indigenous cultural products. Propaganda officials took this responsibility very seriously and issued follow-up directives to both the educational system and the media. Schools and universities were tasked with undertaking patriotic education (Koesel 2020), while traditional and new media were entrusted with promoting cultural confidence (*wenhua zixin*). From a more instrumental point of view, the idea behind indigenous cultural consumption was that it is able to distract citizens from looking for Western cultural products. Those who doubt the importance of ideology in contemporary China should keep in mind that under Xi Jinping safeguarding cultural security (*wenhua anquan*) has been declared to be a component of protecting state security. This reflects the seriousness with which the CCP deals with external cultural influences.

The final adaptation is perhaps the most important, as it concerns the core of the political system. Political pluralism in Eastern Europe put an end to the monopoly of the communist party on power by allowing for the existence of multiple parties. In turn this precipitated the fall of the entire system. The dominant strategy adopted by the CCP to preclude such a development was rival incorporation (Magaloni 2006). To block independent associational life, the CCP absorbed potential challengers like private entrepreneurs (Hou 2019; Koss 2021), religious devotees (Vala 2017), and members of nongovernmental organizations (NGOs) into the party (Xin and Huang 2022), which has doubled in size since 1987, reaching more than ninety-nine million members by the end of 2023 (Zhonggong Zhongyang Zuzhi Bu 2024). Although the strategy of cooptation has not been problem-free, especially with regard to certain ethnic minorities and intellectuals who are critical of the system (Leibold 2020), CCP flexibility in terms of inclusion helps minimize the rise of alternative political movements outside the party. Cumulatively, along with repression (discussed in Section 1.7 and Section 6.2), these four adaptations form the bedrock of the party's post-1989 resilience.

1.6 Implications for Political Reform

When discussing the adaptive responses that the CCP undertook, we should also be mindful that the CCP never tolerated political pluralism. Independent political movements like the China Democracy Party or Charter 08 have been promptly quashed. Analysts have placed faith in the prospect of inner-party democracy and retirement norms to create more transparency and accountability within the party (Manion 1993; Shambaugh 2008) and perhaps as a first step toward some type of softening of the political system. Although there were grounds for such optimism in the 1990s and 2000s, under Xi Jinping any notions of either inner-party democracy or retirement norms have proven to be paper tigers (Fewsmith 2021), especially after Xi secured a norm-breaking third term as general secretary at the Twentieth CCP Congress in 2022.

Other avenues of potential political opening include NGOs, organized religion, and the media. But the regime has made sure that they would not pose a threat to its authority. The scope of operations by NGOs has been reduced to apolitical matters, such as social service provision. Because they are more likely to spread politically harmful ideas, foreign-funded NGOs have been greatly constrained. In addition, organized religious activities have been co-opted by the government through the Sinicization of religion. Some Protestant house churches are allowed to operate (Reny 2018), but only under strict police supervision and as long as they remain small and informal. Turning to the media, we note that although there were some signs of liberalization in the 1990s, and even in the early 2000s, independent journalistic reporting has been extinguished from mainstream print, electronic, and digital media under Xi Jinping. Overall, the avenues that led to political liberalization in other authoritarian states have been closed off in China.

1.7 The Limits of Adaptation: Is Repression the New Normal?

The focus of this Element is on how the four adaptative responses to 1989 have helped to extend the lifespan of the CCP. As we think about the future of China, we should note that each of these adaptations is showing signs of diminishing effectiveness. First, economic reform has generally stalled, with some sectors, like fintech, e-commerce, and ridesharing services, even experiencing a rollback. The anti-corruption campaign has resulted in both the ordinary rich and the tycoons confronting significant property and personal insecurity. It is not clear whether the high levels of growth can be sustained as the state reasserts control over economic activity. Second, the extreme sectoral and geographic inequalities in welfare provision have fueled discontent. This situation is aggravated by the land grabs and demolition of housing by rapacious local governments pursuing lucrative redevelopment projects. Access to housing in the cities and to land in the rural areas are both understood as fundamental welfare rights that cannot be curtailed without resulting in widespread dissatisfaction, which thus far has been directed against the local rather than the central government. But there are no guarantees that the status quo can be preserved indefinitely. Moving to the adaptation of cultural security, recent steps toward limiting access to entertainment targeting effeminate pop stars and computer games may backfire in ways that the censoring of political content has not – in part because the purpose of promoting entertainment is to distract citizens from searching for politically subversive media content. Finally, rival incorporation is facing significant roadblocks in terms of critical intellectuals, ethnic minorities, and Hong Kong citizens.

What are the implications of these trends? The short-term response has been an increase in both physical and digitally facilitated repression. Businesspeople considered insufficiently deferential to the party are either arrested or disappear (Xu 2023), as discussed in Section 2. Welfare protests very rarely result in accommodation or concessions (Dimitrov and Zhang 2021). All types of censorship have increased (Roberts 2018). Furthermore, rivals that cannot be incorporated are subjected to surveillance, detention, incarceration, and persecution (Roberts 2020; Uyghur Tribunal 2021).

A novel feature of the repression in China is the interweaving of high-tech and traditional forms of surveillance to protect political and social order. In 2018, a new initiative of "constructing a peaceful China" (*ping'an Zhongguo jianshe*) was unrolled under the guidance of the CCP Political and Legal Affairs Commission. The aim is to use the feed from surveillance cameras and the intelligence collected through informants to enable grid captains and other grid personnel to maintain law and order, a broad concept that extends from identifying political opponents to solving problems of vagrancy and uncivil behavior. The construction of "peaceful China" has capitalized on the human and technological infrastructure that undergirded the 2.498 million grids (*wangge*) that extended through China's urban and rural territory as of 2019. It also reinvigorated foundational Maoist ideas of mass mobilization for public security work (known as "the Fengqiao experience"), whose current instantiation involves CCP-sanctioned grassroot vigilantism and the collection of intelligence through "peaceful China" volunteer groups (Zhongyang Zhengfawei Bangongting 2021a; 2021b). The decision in 2023 to create a Social Work Department under the CCP will further strengthen these initiatives, as this department will be in charge of guiding grassroots party building, social govern-ance, and managing social volunteers, including informants.

Is repression the new normal? The COVID-19 pandemic has complicated the answer to this question, as it justified further crackdowns on freedom of expression and assembly under the guise of protecting public health. With the ending of zero-COVID in 2023, a pressing question was whether the hardening of the repressive system enabled by the pandemic would persist in the post-COVID-19 period. Although ubiquitous surveillance, artificial intelligence (AI) policing, and social order blacklists are here to stay (Arsène 2019; Jee 2022; Kim and Lorentzen 2023), we must also be mindful that repression is not sustainable as a long-term governance strategy. This means that, for the CCP to stay in power, it will either have to develop new adaptations or it will need to go down a path of gradual political liberalization.

1.8 Structure of the Element

This introductory section is followed by four sections that discuss respectively the main adaptive responses deployed by the CCP in the aftermath of 1989: economic liberalization; welfare expansion; cultural security; and rival incorp-oration. Each section analyzes how the specific adaptation has contributed to resilience. In addition, each section deals with the question of whether the utility of the adaptive response has reached its end. The concluding section revisits China's impressive record of resilience but also highlights signs showing that the adaptive capacity of the party is waning. This final section summarizes the lessons from the CCP's controlled adaptation and outlines pathways for a potential malfunctioning of the strategies to achieve resilience following the shock of 1989. As a whole, this Element sheds light on the adaptive responses that have allowed the CCP to persist to this day and provides an assessment of their capacity to ensure CCP longevity in the future.

2 Economic Reform

Reforming inefficient centrally planned economies requires several important steps. One is allowing the market to coexist with the plan and eventually to displace it as the main coordinating mechanism of economic activity. Another is initially tolerating and eventually legally sanctioning private entrepreneur-ial activity. Finally, attracting foreign capital and technology significantly helps boost productivity. Prior to 1989, China had started to grow out of the plan (Naughton 1995), allowing de facto private economic activity, especially in the township and village enterprises (TVEs) (Oi 1999; Tsai 2007; Dickson 2008; Huang 2008), and attracting substantial foreign direct investment (FDI)

(Gallagher 2005). However, no progress was made on the most consequential decision facing a communist regime with a centrally planned economy, namely when and how to reform SOEs. The initial legal framework that would allow for enterprise bankruptcy was passed in 1986 (Heilmann 2011, 105), but the Tiananmen Square protests (which were partly driven by socioeconomic uncertainties) slowed down overall economic reform and, especially, the restructuring of state-owned industry. SOE reform was a politically explosive task with an uncertain outcome that the party was not able to confront until after 1989.

This section first provides a general discussion about how centrally planned economies approach the problem of restructuring state-owned property. It then evaluates the contribution of the private sector to Chinese economic activity. Subsequently, we turn to an examination of the two decades of cooperative business–state relations, spanning the period from Deng Xiaoping's 1992 Southern Tour (which reinforced China's commitment to the market economy) to Xi Jinping's assumption of power in 2012. Xi introduced a new, more rigid attitude toward business, which is discussed in Section 2.4. He also imprisoned some tycoons and took moves against the most powerful technology companies. These actions may seem puzzling, but as we explain in the remainder of this section, they are consistent with the logic of protecting the interests of the party and its top leadership. Nevertheless, they also have the potential of alienating large segments of the superrich who are experiencing property and personal insecurity. We end with the implications of the reassertion of CCP control over economic activities for the future of the Chinese political model, especially with regard to the willingness of private entrepreneurs to oppose the party-state.

2.1 Comparative Perspectives on Reforming State-Owned Firms in Centrally Planned Economies

China is not unique in terms of the challenges it faced in connection with its economic reforms. Such challenges have emerged in all communist regimes with centrally planned economies. In the 1990s, following the prescriptions of the Washington Consensus, the formerly socialist Eastern European regimes undertook rapid privatization of state-owned industrial assets (Orenstein 2001). Two negative side effects accompanied this process. One was the extraordinary social costs in the form of layoffs and loss of welfare entitlements (Cook 1993), thereby making the reforms extremely unpopular (Ost 2006). Another was the powerholders' loss of control over state assets. In extreme cases, this led to state capture (Freeland 2000; Klebnikov 2000; Hoffman 2002; Dimitrov 2017).

After closely studying the Eastern European reform experience, China was committed to minimizing the social costs of the transition and to preventing the rise of oligarchs who could hold the party hostage (Weber 2021; Zhang 2021). Executing these twin goals required careful planning, thus delaying the reforms by nearly a decade. It was not until 1997 that SOE restructuring began in earnest. Even then, no Eastern European-style big-bang approach was implemented. The CCP remained in charge of the process, spearheading enterprise transformation into shareholding companies (corporatization) and subsequently allowing partial privatization of smaller SOEs. This stands in marked contrast to the plunder of state resources that took place in Russia in the 1990s. Delaying the start of privatization and carefully managing it once it was underway also meant that the regime was able to limit the social costs of the market transition. Although there was discontent among those who had been laid off without receiving adequate compensation (Hurst 2009), the extent of dissatisfaction was manageable in comparison to the worker protests and strikes that erupted throughout the former Eastern Bloc during the implementation of shock therapy in the 1990s (Ost 2006).

Although China proved to be more adept in its integration with the global economy than Eastern Europe, its entry into the WTO in 2001 presented some challenges. Economic activity became significantly more rule-bound (Steinfeld 2010), yet protectionism survived in various forms. Foreigners faced numerous onerous requirements when attempting to provide services like banking, insurance, and telecommunications. Strategic sectors, such as mining and the extractive industries, as well as certain types of manufacturing, were also protected. Subsidies were provided to agriculture, fisheries, and large industrial enterprises. Unveiled in 2015, the Made in China 2025 (*Zhongguo Zhizao 2025*) initiative further extended protection to the high-tech sectors, such as information technology, robotics, green vehicles, aerospace engineering, and new materials (United States Office of the Trade Representative 2023). The party took an activist approach to the Chinese economy, managing firms that were entrusted with national security functions. Growing securitization and civil–military fusion (Pearson, Rithmire, and Tsai 2023) also meant shielding firms from foreign competition.

2.2 The Size of the Private Economy

Considering that the economic reforms were introduced more than four decades ago, we should be able to provide information about the size of the private sector. Xi Jinping has publicized one set of numbers, which indicate that the private sector accounts for more than 50 percent of tax receipts, 60 percent of GDP, 70 percent of innovation, 80 percent of urban employment, and 90 percent of enterprises (Zhonggong Zhongyang Zuzhi Bu 2021b, 523). The problem with such statistics is that they lack clarity in terms of the meaning of "private": it can refer to general categories such as civilian-run enterprises (*minying qiye*) or nonstate firms (*fei gongyouzhi qiye*), which then can be further subdivided into a broad array of firms ranging from sole proprietorships (*geti gongshang hu*) to privately owned firms (*siying qiye*) and Hong Kong, Macau, Taiwan, and foreign-invested firms (*gang'ao taishang/waishang qiye*). To complicate matters further, there may be privately owned companies that have been spun off from conglomerates known as business groups (*qiye jituan*), even though the parent remains state-owned (Keister 2000; Oi 2011, 6). Under Xi Jinping, the party has promoted the idea of "mixed ownership," which involves a mutual fusion of state, collective, and nonpublic capital (Pearson, Rithmire, and Tsai 2020, 15). In light of these definitional challenges, it is difficult to produce precise estimates of the size of the private sector in China. Perhaps more important than the exact contribution of nonstate businesses to the economy is how the CCP has approached SOEs and nonstate firms since 1989.

2.3 Cooperative Party–Business Relations, 1992–2012

We can make several general observations about party–business relations from Deng's 1992 Southern Tour to Xi Jinping's assumption of power in 2012. First, state-owned firms remained a priority. This means that they continued to receive extensive support from the government. Although they were corporatized following passage of the Company Law in 1993 and partially privatized after the Fifteenth Party Congress in 1997, they continued to benefit from financial injections through the state banking system, the State Asset Supervision Administration of China (SASAC), and local asset supervision administrations. The desire to create national champions means that business groups that emerged from the SOEs continued to receive extensive government support even after China's 2001 entry into the WTO. Second, technology companies, many of which had been established with overseas venture capital, also benefited from government support in the form of limiting and eventually blocking Western competitors from market access. Third, small firms were exposed to a survival-of-the-fittest model. The TVEs, which had been the engine of growth prior to 1989, were either privatized or went bankrupt. Single proprietorships and small private firms found it difficult to obtain bank loans, but most were able to survive and adapt. FDI continued to flow in. Although it favored the SOEs, the party played the role of a general facilitator over a wide range of entrepreneurial activity.

Most remarkable about this period is that, even though business grew substantially, it did not challenge the party-state. Major SOEs and large private companies enjoyed a cooperative relationship with the government. The powerful military–business complex was placed under civilian control (Mulvenon 2001). Billionaires began to emerge in the 1990s and their number increased throughout the 2000s (Zhang 2021). The superrich were co-opted by the party with positions on local- and central-level legislative bodies and were largely left to enjoy their wealth (Hou 2019; Zhang 2021; Xu 2023). Although corruption thrived, it was conducive to growth (Wedeman 2012; Ang 2016; 2020). Businesspeople were no democrats, as they expressed no interest in opposing the party-state, which was allowing them to prosper (Dickson 2003; 2008; Tsai 2007). Both sides thus benefited from a symbiotic relationship in which the state facilitated business success and in turn business delivered the high levels of GDP growth that were essential for a party whose legitimacy was closely tied to economic performance. This equilibrium would change once Xi Jinping assumed power.

2.4 Party–Business Relations under Xi Jinping

Perhaps the most notable feature of business–government relations under Xi Jinping is that the party has become directly involved in the management of nonstate firms. Although the initial indicia of the transition to this hands-on approach emerged before the 2010s, the Xi administration made it clear that this was the new normal. This led scholars to update their descriptions of the essence of business–government relations in the 2010s. Specifically, whereas the pre-2012 period and the first two years of the Xi administration are characterized as "state capitalism" (Naughton and Tsai 2015; Kurlantzick 2016), the post-2015 era is described as "party-state capitalism" (Blanchette 2020; Pearson, Rithmire, and Tsai 2020; 2023) in order to capture the shift from state *dirigisme* to capitalism "more directly in the service of the party's political survival" (Pearson, Rithmire, and Tsai 2020, 6).

The establishment of party cells in private firms is the most palpable indicator of CCP interest in becoming involved in the management of private business. Of particular note are situations in which the party secretary and the firm president (or chair of the board) are the same person (see Section 5 of this Element).

Other mechanisms of control are less direct but nevertheless highly effective. First, scholars have noted the financialization of government institutions, which allows the state to have influence over both SOEs and nonstate firms by purchasing minority shares through vehicles such as state capital investment and operations companies (*guoyou ziben touzi, yunying gongsi*) as well as industrial guidance funds (*chanye yindao jijin*) (Naughton 2020, 64–66). A second mechanism of control came with the creation of special management shares that gave the party-state leverage over technology giants like Alibaba, Tencent, and Baidu (Pearson, Rithmire, and Tsai 2020, 12). Government oversight offices at nonstate firms are a third mechanism of control and a concrete manifestation of the rise of the "investor state" in the 2010s (Chen and Rithmire 2020).

Scholars have pointed out that additional evidence of the party–business nexus is provided by the fact that private firms have been called upon to carry out strategic tasks such as surveillance, social credit, and poverty alleviation, whose successful execution is directly related to the paramount goal of stability maintenance (Pearson, Rithmire, and Tsai 2020). Nonstate firms have displayed a willingness to collaborate with the regime on issues that range from censorship (Gallagher and Miller 2021; Ruan et al. 2021) to fintech regulation (Jing Wang 2021). Companies that have resisted, like Ant Financial, have been punished. From the vantage point of 2024, it is clear that Xi Jinping is interested in using all firms, regardless of ownership type, to advance his vision of promoting the strategic sectors, including environmental protection, new energy, biotechnology, and information systems. This grand steerage fits nicely with the economic and technological self-sufficiency projects, such as dual circulation (*guonei guoji shuang xunhuan*) and Made in China 2025 (García Herrero 2021; Naughton 2020). To remain successful, firms must support those party initiatives.

2.5 An Aggressive Turn: The Assault on Tech and Alienation of the Superrich

The general understanding of business–government relations in contemporary China is that they are symbiotic and that therefore neither ordinary entrepreneurs nor the superrich would benefit from challenging the primacy of the CCP that has allowed them to accumulate wealth (Tsai 2007; Dickson 2008; Hou 2019; Zhang 2021). Although this is a reasonable argument, two recent trends call into question the ongoing capacity of the party-state to maintain this equilibrium. One is the assault on platform companies and the other is the arrest and imprisonment of several high-profile tycoons.

The regulatory crackdown on technology companies took place in 2020–21 and affected major firms like Alibaba, Tencent, JD.com, Didi, and Meituan. These cases have been highly publicized, so we can review them briefly here. First, the IPO of Alibaba's Ant Financial was blocked following public criticism by Jack Ma, the main founder of the Alibaba Group, of the Chinese financial regulatory system. Second, tech giant Tencent lost significant share value when the government blocked its planned foray into online education and limited its computer games business. Furthermore, the ride-hailing company Didi was the subject of a regulatory probe after it listed overseas, and the delivery company Meituan was investigated on anticompetitiveness grounds. Cumulatively, the crackdown erased US$1.5 trillion in value from the stocks of the affected companies (*The Economist* 2022).

These costly decisions may appear to be irrational, but deeper investigation reveals their logic. Ant Financial assumed the functions of a banking institution without insuring itself against financial risk. Considering that it rapidly amassed 15 percent of all outstanding consumer loans in China, a potential default would have created heightened risk for political instability (*The Economist* 2022). Tencent's plans to expand into education infringed on the party's monopoly over the ideological sphere, which includes the education sector (see Section 4 of this Element). The conglomerate's venture into online games also clashed with the party's desire to limit the time Chinese citizens spend playing computer games. Finally, Didi angered the party by seeking foreign rather than domestic financing. Although the assault on tech appeared to have eased off in 2022 and 2023, the 2020–21 episode had clear significance, namely, the party was sending a costly signal to the platform industry that it could not set its own rules. Quite the opposite: tech was required to respect the regulatory framework put in place by the communist party. In addition, platform companies were expected to engage in R&D and engineering innovation rather than in perfecting their online business model. A case in point is Baidu, best known for its search engine, which was awarded China's first driverless ride-hailing license (*The Economist* 2022). The CCP, not the tech companies, is in the driver's seat.

The second episode is the arrest of high-profile tycoons. Although no precise tally is available, one scholar estimates that between 2008 and 2017 one-fifth of the 124 tycoons in his sample were convicted, detained, or implicated in corruption (Xu 2023, 610). Some additional features of this phenomenon can be discerned from both Chinese and Western accounts that have emerged about it in the past decade. Even if officially these billionaires are brought to justice because they are corrupt, a closer look reveals two patterns. One involves individuals who were part of the networks of disgraced or retired politicians. An example is Whitney Duan (Duan Weihong), who was close to the family of former Premier Wen Jiabao and to fallen Chongqing Party Secretary Sun Zhengcai (Shum 2021). Another is the case of Xiao Jianhua, a "banker to the elite," who was abducted by mainland state security officials from the Four Seasons Hotel in Hong Kong in 2017 and was sentenced to thirteen years of imprisonment for financial crimes in 2022.[1] Xiao is rumored to have been close to the Jiang Zemin leadership faction. The case of Guo Wengui/Miles Kwok, who escaped a certain arrest in China by moving to New York City (where he

---

[1] www.wsj.com/articles/vanished-chinese-billionaire-set-to-face-criminal-trial-in-shanghai-11654787300.

enjoyed the high life for a decade, until he was eventually convicted of defrauding investors in 2024), is another illustration of the sorry fate that awaits tycoons whose patrons (in his case Vice-Minister of State Security Ma Jian) lose power. This may explain why Wang Jianlin, who was once dubbed the richest man in Asia, built broad networks that involve both politicians who are currently in power and leaders who have retired (Forsythe 2015). Wang's real-estate and entertainment fortune has decreased in recent years, but he remains free, unlike other prominent tycoons who backed the wrong elite faction.

The other oligarchs who have suffered under Xi Jinping are those who were imprisoned for being outspoken. Two cases, both handled in 2020–21, are relevant here: one is the case of real-estate mogul Ren Zhiqiang and the other is the case of the pig- and chicken-farming billionaire Sun Dawu. Both men were sentenced to eighteen-year prison terms, Ren in 2020 on charges of corruption and Sun in 2021 for "picking quarrels and provoking trouble." But both had also irked the CCP, one by challenging Xi Jinping's handling of the COVID-19 pandemic (Ren) and the other by talking about democracy (Sun) (British Broadcasting Corporation 2020; 2021).

What lessons can we draw from these illustrative cases? All of these tycoons were likely corrupt, but corruption is not the reason for their imprisonment. The CCP has been waging anti-corruption struggles since the 1930s, when it controlled only the revolutionary base areas, which constituted no more than 1 percent of the territory of China (Carothers 2022). Corruption is an essential ingredient of China's economic model (Ang 2016; 2020), which means that any leader who is genuinely committed to stamping it out risks a severe slowdown in growth (Wang and Yan 2020), with potential system-destabilizing effects. As these exemplary cases make clear, tycoons fall when they back the wrong faction or when they are too outspoken.

The pressing question we need to address here is whether the tycoons who remain free will continue to tolerate the CCP's noncooperative behavior. The short-term response of tycoons who are not imprisoned has been to engage in philanthropy and to endorse the party's priorities, like poverty alleviation. For example, Jack Ma became devoted to such good works in 2021 (Ding 2021), after the scuttled Ant IPO, thus providing a parallel to the Russian oligarchs in the 2000s who were able to survive Putin's ascent to power (Frye 2006). However, as comparative research establishes, oligarchs are keen to defend their wealth when their fortunes are threatened (Winters 2011; Markus 2015), and philanthropy may not be the most effective strategy for protecting property and personal security. How much longer will tycoons like Jack Ma continue to do good works and contribute to charity? Will the superrich organize to challenge the state? Might they try to convert their economic prowess into political power?

Two possible answers can be provided to this question. One is suggested by arguments about the existence of a mafia-state in contemporary China, where business and government hold each other in check through an equilibrium described as "mutual endangerment" (Rithmire and Chen 2021; Rithmire 2023). Similarly, scholars stress the "mutual dependence and vulnerability" that exists between firms and the CCP (Pearson, Rithmire, and Tsai 2023, 39). These interpretations give significant agency to entrepreneurs. This may be true subnationally, but at the central level the capacity of even the richest tycoons to exercise control over government officials is questionable. To put this in perspective, we may think of other mafia-states, like those that existed in Russia and some Eastern European countries like Bulgaria in the 1990s (Klebnikov 2000; Ganev 2007). In those cases, business literally captured the state and either ensconced itself in the Kremlin (during Yeltsin's second term as president, 1996–99) or installed a government that ruled on its behalf (in the mid-1990s in Bulgaria). Importantly, China is far removed from this type of situation. The state has the upper hand and has adeptly avoided capture (Zhang 2021). In contrast to the postcommunist regimes in the 1990s, in which central authority was weak, the CCP remains very strong. Its noncooperative relations with platform companies and its imprisonment of troublemaking tycoons are concrete manifestations of such strength. They send a clear signal that those who do not follow the party line will be punished. Thus, the options of the superrich are limited to complying with party diktat or risking both their wealth and their liberty.

2.6 Whither Economic Reform in China?

This section has reviewed China's impressive record of economic reform, demonstrating that optimistic pronouncements about the end of history notwithstanding (Fukuyama 1989), there is no necessary link between marketization and democratization. The experience of China also shows that the Harvard Plan of shock therapy involving rapid privatization and marketization is not the only pathway out of central planning. By delaying reform of the SOEs, China was able to minimize the social costs of market transition that were poorly received by the citizenry in Eastern Europe. Finally, the case of China shows that privatization need not lead to the state's wholesale loss of control over its assets. In contrast to Eastern Europe, the party-state in China was able to retain substantial leverage over the SOEs that were only partially privatized.

This section has also demonstrated that, in contrast to dominant theorizing in comparative politics, Chinese entrepreneurs are no democrats. Businesspeople benefited from being loyal supporters of the CCP in the 1980s, 1990s, and the 2000s. They were able to accumulate extraordinary levels of wealth while at the same time helping the party achieve the legitimacy-generating economic growth that it needed. No rational entrepreneur would risk disturbing this beneficial relationship by calling for political reform.

The Xi era has presented a new chapter in business–government relations, in which the CCP is much less cooperative toward companies that do not fully support its strategic vision for economic development and toward tycoons who either back the wrong elite faction or express overt criticism of the party. Combined with the now permanent anti-corruption campaign, such steps by the party have had a sobering effect on entrepreneurs. The long-term impact on China's economic trajectory remains to be seen.

3 Extending the Social Safety Net

A standard notion among scholars is that communist regimes, which are understood as "shortage economies" (Kornai 1980), do not seek to satisfy the consumption needs and welfare preferences of the population (Friedrich and Brzezinski 1965). Instead, some argue, they rule by repressing the masses and rewarding the elites (Arendt 1951; Bueno de Mesquita at al. 2003). This received wisdom was challenged both by early scholarship that emphasizes the decline in repression in the post-Stalinist regimes (Dallin and Breslauer 1970) and by subsequent studies of the social contract arguing that citizens will remain quiescent for as long as the regime provides them with stable access to jobs, housing, welfare benefits, and consumer goods (Millar 1985; Hauslohner 1987; Cook 1993). The collapse of the Soviet and the Eastern European communist regimes led to an archival revolution that has allowed scholars to assess the validity of arguments about centrally planned economies that were developed without access to primary regime-generated sources. Recent archival studies confirm the insights in the earlier literature on the importance that communist regimes attach to satisfying the consumption preferences of the population (Betts 2010; Dimitrov 2018). Research on welfare dictatorships has thus validated Václav Havel's astute observation that late socialism involved "the coming together of a dictatorship and a consumer society" (Havel 1979, 71).

Against this theoretical background, we can see the events of 1989 in a new light. One reason for the Tiananmen unrest was worker uncertainty about how they might be affected by the bankruptcies of urban enterprises that would inevitably accompany the transition from plan to market (Walder and Gong 1991). This section discusses why, in response to welfare-driven discontent in 1989, the party delayed the reform of inefficient urban industrial enterprises until the second half of the 1990s. A market social contract was gradually unrolled in the 1990s and 2000s. Benefits like healthcare and pensions, which under Mao had been reserved primarily for urban workers, were extended nearly universally throughout the country. This major expansion was driven by the imperative of stability maintenance, which emerged as a central concern following the domestic and international shocks of 1989. Yet, as this section argues, the social contract operates efficiently only when citizens sensitize the authorities to their grievances through the complaints system and when the regime demonstrates a sufficient level of responsiveness. A worrying trend in this regard is the decline in citizen complaints and the corresponding increase in protests, which began in the 2000s and became entrenched by the 2010s. Under Xi, widespread socioeconomic contention has been met with repression, leading to a crisis in responsiveness. The implications of such a crisis for regime stability are discussed in the conclusion to this section.

3.1 The Changing Nature of the Social Contract in Post-Mao China

In the lead-up to the 1989 Tiananmen events, efforts were made to reform the inefficient socialist social contract, which extended costly cradle-to-grave benefits to urban workers and their families (Dillon 2015). Worker discontent about high inflation and the legal sanctioning of enterprise bankruptcy and unemployment paused the implementation of welfare-reducing urban reforms. The central government continued to supply SOEs with sufficient funds to maintain and even expand their pre-1989 workforce, so the number of individuals employed by state-owned units (*guoyou danwei*) grew from 103 million in 1989 to 112 million in 1994 (*Zhongguo tongji nianjian* 2010, 118). Consumer price subsidies also increased substantially, from 31.7 billion yuan in 1988 to 71.2 billion yuan in 1998 (*Xin Zhongguo* 1999, 12). The dismantling of the socialist social contract for urban workers did not begin until after the 1997 Fifteenth Party Congress, when the policy of "grasping the large and letting go of the small" (*zhuada fangxiao*) authorized privatization of smaller SOEs and a drastic reduction in their workforce. This decade-long delay of reform was economically inefficient but politically expedient.

Learning from Eastern Europe, where enterprise restructuring resulted in a massive rise in unemployment, China implemented SOE reform gradually. Workers were initially classified as "laid off" (*xiagang*) rather than immediately becoming unemployed. For three years, these laid-off workers maintained a relationship with their work unit, drew a salary, received benefits, and engaged in retraining. It was only after the three-year period that those workers still seeking employment were reclassified as unemployed (Tang and Yang 2008). Despite these efforts to cushion SOE employees, there was still significant discontent about the loss of benefits and entitlements (Hurst 2009). A policy that was meant to ease the transition to a post-socialist social contract was put in place whereby workers were allowed to purchase at below-market rates subsidized housing provided to them by their work units. The late 1990s also inaugurated the *dibao* (minimum-living guarantee), which in principle supplies means-tested financial assistance to those who are worst affected by the transition, though more instrumental stability-maintenance considerations also appear to have been at work (Pan 2020; Solinger 2022).

In general, the 2000s and 2010s witnessed a systematic expansion of benefits. The New Rural Cooperative Medical System (*xinxing nongcun hezuo yiliao zhidu*) was introduced in 2002 as a way to reduce illness-related poverty among rural *hukou* (household registration) holders (Klotzbücher et al. 2010). The Labor Contract Law, passed in 2008, stipulates that all employees are entitled to a labor contract. To the extent that it was properly enforced, this law made it more difficult for employers to fire workers without cause, to maintain forced labor conditions, to delay the payment of wages, and to avoid making benefit contributions. The 2010 Social Security Law mandates that both employers and employees must make contributions to five different types of social insurance: pensions, medical insurance, work-related injury insurance, unemployment insurance, and maternity insurance. Although the law represents a step in the right direction, several serious problems remain: great inter- and intra-provincial variation in the extent of coverage of the various social insurance schemes (Huang 2020); non-transferability of benefits and entitlements from one location to another; and incomplete implementation and coverage, especially for migrant workers in cities, for urban residents without fixed employment, and for residents of rural areas (Frazier 2010; Huang 2015). Despite these shortcomings, the gradual expansion of welfare benefits that has taken place during the last two decades has been a point of pride for the CCP (Wang Jingqing 2021, 90). For this reason, the 2023 drop in the number of citizens with health insurance due to rising costs was not welcome news for the party (Sun 2023).

Historically, urban–rural inequality has been exacerbated by the existence of a two-track social benefits system, whereby urban residents receive substantially higher benefits than rural residents (Gao 2010). The situation is especially problematic for those rural migrants who have worked in the cities for long periods of time but who still possess a rural *hukou*, which only entitles them to rural pensions that are inadequate for survival in the urban areas. Established in the 1950s as a form of social control (Wang 2005), the *hukou* greatly reduced rural-to-urban mobility in the 1950–70s. Although migration to the cities became very common in the post-Mao period, those who held a rural *hukou* were excluded from the urban welfare state. In recent years, many localities have abolished restrictions on the acquisition of urban *hukou*. Some have allowed rural *hukou* holders to purchase property in urban areas, thus making them eligible to access state-managed urban schools, which generally provide higher-quality education than the private schools to which the children of migrants are typically relegated. However, currently available data do not allow us to ascertain how widespread these changes have been (for an important contribution, see Vortherms 2024).

In sum, as China was moving from a socialist to a market social contract, the scope of the contract initially contracted but was eventually expanded, reaching levels that surpassed provision under Mao, especially with regard to rural residents who did not receive pensions under central planning. Though more generous than its counterpart under central planning, the post-Mao welfare state must further improve benefits. The reason is that public goods provision is a central pillar of regime legitimacy in China (Dickson 2016, 11) and citizens overwhelmingly feel that this is the responsibility of the government rather than of individuals (Dickson 2016, 189).

3.2 Sensitizing the Regime to Citizen Preferences Regarding the Social Contract

In competitive authoritarian regimes, elections can apprise the leadership about citizen preferences with regard to the social contract. China uses nonelectoral mechanisms to assess these preferences. One channel for studying public opinion is analysis of the content of citizen petitions (*xinfang*), which focus primarily on citizen dissatisfaction with fulfilment of the social contract. *Xinfang* have emerged as the main mechanism for the transmission of information in communist regimes. Protests are also informative, but this information is disseminated both vertically and horizontally (Lorentzen 2017), in contrast to petitions, which are private requests for services that are transmitted only vertically. Since the 1990s, the Internet has provided an additional avenue for citizens to communicate their views – posting on websites and social media under their real names (Distelhorst and Hou 2017). Like protests, Internet posts allow for a public airing of grievances, thus calling for a different response from that issued in reaction to citizen complaints. From the point of view of regime insiders, complaints provide the most effective mechanism for learning about citizen grievances because the information is transmitted only vertically, rather than both vertically and horizontally as in the case of protests and Internet posts (Dimitrov 2023).

Petition reports, which have existed since the Mao period (Shanghai Municipal Archives 1965), supply leaders with statistical data on the number of petitions, the breakdown of petitions into different categories (labor protection, welfare concerns, legal matters), and the social characteristics of the petitioners. These reports are prepared with different frequencies, at the level of the county,[2] the province (*Tianjin* 1997, 311), and nationally (Zhonggong Zhongyang Guojia Jiguan 2008, 1083). In addition to petition reporting, leaders can assess public opinion on the social contract through other avenues as well, such as opinion polling (*Gaige Neican* 2014a) and reports on protests, which are variously referred to as mass incidents (*quntixing shijian*) (*Gaige Neican* 2014b) or sudden incidents (*tufa shijian*) (*Gaige Neican* 2012). Although some have argued that negative news is suppressed in certain types of reporting (Pan and Chen 2018), the leadership is aware of the potential of withholding information and it actively works to mitigate such problems by fostering redundancy, thus allowing for a cross-checking of intelligence received through different reporting streams (Dimitrov 2023; Gao 2016). In short, Chinese leaders have access to multiple channels to assess citizen perceptions about the fulfilment of the social contract. The problem, as we will discuss in the remainder of this section, is that citizens today are complaining less and are increasingly likely to engage in protests.

3.2.1 Complaints to the Authorities 1989–2004

In the wake of the Tiananmen Square protests, as the top Chinese leaders were dealing with crises that threatened the very core of China's political model, they also found time to think about citizen complaints, the number of which had declined in the years leading up to 1989, despite the clear and objective deterioration in the economic well-being of urban workers. Comments were made in the summer of 1989 about providing prompt and detailed responses to citizen complaints by top leaders, such as Shanghai mayor Zhu Rongji, General Secretary Jiang Zemin, Politburo Standing Committee member Qiao Shi, and Premier Li Peng (*Renmin Xinfang* 1989a; 1989c). A further indicator of the importance of petitions was a meeting of ten directors of provincial-level letters-and-visits bureaus convened by the top leadership in August 1989 (*Renmin Xinfang* 1989b) and a September 1989 notice to all provincial-level party and government offices by the Central Bureau of Letters and Visits regarding strengthening complaints work (*Renmin Xinfang* 1990). The focus on the system of citizen petitions is not surprising, considering that it provides

---

[2] Interview with letters and visits office bureaucrat, Zouping, China, July 29, 2011.

an essential channel to regain the trust of the masses through increased respon-siveness to popular grievances.

The effect of this attention by the top echelon of the party-state was an increase in the number of letters and visits, thus reintegrating citizens into the system (see Figure 1). In the 1990s petitions came primarily from rural residents who were expressing dissatisfaction with the excessive taxation, high compulsory procurement quotas, cadre malfeasance, and corrupt imple-mentation of village elections. By the early 2000s, most petitions were initi-ated by unemployed urban workers, who sought to express dissatisfaction with enterprise restructuring and were demanding social welfare payments and poverty relief. The number of complaints increased very rapidly, and by 2004 it stood at 13.7 million, more than double the 5.5 million petitions received in 1990 (see Figure 1).

3.2.2 Decline in Complaints Received by the Letters-and-Visits Bureaus since 2005

The number of petitions handled by the *xinfang* offices declined after 2004 (see Figure 1). The frequency of complaints has been low not only in absolute terms but also in relative terms: at 4 per 1,000 people, the rate of complaints in 2019 was nearly an order of magnitude smaller than the lowest volume of complaints in communist Bulgaria, which stood at 36.67 per 1,000 people at its nadir in

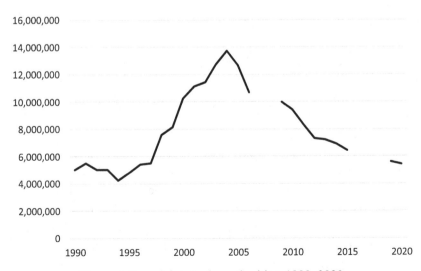

Figure 1 Complaints to the authorities, 1990–2020.

Source: Author's dataset, constructed from provincial yearbooks and materials for internal circulation.

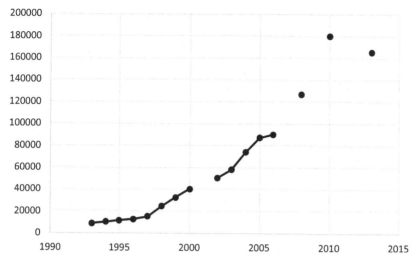

Figure 2 Mass incidents, 1993–2013.

Source: Author's dataset, based on Wedeman 2009, Sun 2011, Zhang and Chen 2014, and on materials for internal circulation.

1987 (Dimitrov 2023). What is especially worrisome about the decline registered in Figure 1 is that it has occurred in conjunction with a dramatic increase in the frequency of mass incidents, mostly at the subnational level (see Figure 2). Participation in mass incidents indicates that citizens do not believe that their grievances can be resolved through the formal complaint channels that are available at the local levels. Despite attempts to incentivize citizens to stop protesting and to utilize the letters-and-visits system (Zhonggong Zhongyang Bangongting 2014), socioeconomic contention has persisted. When Xi Jinping assumed power, there was a new urgency to handle protests in a manner that would maintain social stability, a paramount concern since the 1989 Tiananmen protests.

3.3 Declining Responsiveness to Citizen Grievances

How responsive has the leadership been to citizen preferences? Here we need to draw a distinction between macro-level responsiveness by top leaders and micro-level grassroots responsiveness. Data on leadership response are difficult to come by, but they can be found in internal government publications. An annual report of the National Administration for Letters and Visits reveals, for example, that Politburo Standing Committee members issued instructions on 90 percent of the reports on trends in the letters and phone calls (*xindian qingkuang*) that they received throughout 2007 (Zhonggong Zhongyang Guojia Jiguan 2008, 1083).

We also have specific evidence that Jiang Zemin (*Renmin Xinfang* 2000a), Zhu Rongji (*Renmin Xinfang* 2000b), and Hu Jintao and Wen Jiabao (Zhonggong Zhongyang Guojia Jiguan 2008, 1084) have all issued instructions on citizen complaints. This surprisingly high level of responsiveness bespeaks the value that leaders attach to the monitoring of petitions. Major legislative change, such as abolition of the agricultural tax in 2006, promulgation of the Labor Contract Law in 2008, and expansion of the social safety net in the 2000s and 2010s, can be directly traced to citizen grievances expressed either through complaints or protests. Internal government publications emphasize that responsiveness is essential to safeguard trust in communist party cadres (*Lingdao Canyue* 2014), to maintain social stability (Lin and Liu 2008, 3; *Lingdao Canyue* 2013), and to prevent collective protests (Ningxia 2019, 193; Sichuan 2019, 80; Hainan 2020, 121–123).

The biggest challenge for the center has been the low micro-level responsiveness of local governments to citizen grievances, as indicated by the increasing number of mass incidents (protests). Further discussion of this trend will be provided in Section 3.3.1.

3.3.1 The New Normal: Protest Responses After 2012

China is often hailed as a *sui generis* authoritarian regime. One apposite example is the incidence and handling of protests. In other autocracies, protests are rare events that can lead to regime destabilization (Kuran 1991; Lohmann 1994) and thus they are resolutely suppressed. This parallels the handling of political dissent in China, which is rare but harshly repressed, given its capacity to threaten stability (Perry 2002, ix–xxxii). Where China stands out, however, is in the frequency and responsiveness to socioeconomic contention: there were well over one million collective incidents in 1990–2012, yet the regime did not unravel. Moreover, instead of repression, socioeconomic protests (rightful resistance) were likely to be met with toleration and even accommodation (O'Brien and Li 2006; Tong and Lei 2014; Elfstrom 2019; Li 2019; Elfstrom 2021), especially when they were large-scale, disruptive, and took place in urban areas (Cai 2010; Chen 2012).[3] Why does such toleration occur? One claim is that the center welcomes protests, as they help alleviate higher-level leaders' information problems regarding local-level malfeasance (Lorentzen 2013). Another argument, consistent with the emphasis of this Element on responsiveness, is that the regime increases its level of support by appearing to be accountable to popular demands (Lee and Zhang 2013; Heurlin 2016). Therefore, some have posited that protests are not only compatible with but are

---

[3] Nationalist protests were also likely to be accommodated (Weiss 2014).

even necessary to ensure stability (Chen 2012). In sum, scholars stress that the typical post-1989 protest is not repressed as it is not a source of concern for the leadership. China thus emerges as an exceptional case of an autocracy that is tolerant of socioeconomic protests.

Existing research on protest toleration referenced in the preceding paragraph does not use empirical data that go beyond 2012 (see Göbel 2019 and Zhang and Pan 2019 for exceptions). In light of the general toughening of policies under Xi Jinping, a question emerges whether attitudes toward contentious activity have changed as well. We can address this issue by analyzing over 65,000 cases of socioeconomic protest that took place between November 2013 and June 2016 (Dimitrov and Zhang 2021). Our results reveal a radical change in attitudes toward contention under Xi. Accommodation has been very rare, even when the protests were large-scale or disruptive (occurring in less than 1 percent of 2,604 such cases in the Dimitrov and Zhang dataset). Instead, our analysis reveals that the overwhelming response has been repression. What explains this? Several long-term trends, all of which precede Xi's assumption of power, converged by 2012–13, leading to a harsher party-state response to protests.

The first development was technological change, which facilitated protest organizing. Chinese leaders had become sensitized to the fact that cell phones had enabled coordination during Arab Spring in 2010–11 and the anti-Putin demonstrations in 2012 (*Neibu Canyue* 2013a; 2013b). By 2012–13, the overwhelming majority of Internet users in China were accessing the Internet through mobile devices, allowing them to exchange information in real time and making it easier for online contention to spill off-line (Xie 2013). This is also confirmed by our dataset (Dimitrov and Zhang 2021), in which the single most powerful predictor of protest incidence is the number of Internet users in individual Chinese provinces (r-squared of 0.88 in a bivariate regression and t=14.82 for 2014). Concerns had been mounting about the rapidity with which contentious episodes could be organized with the help of mobile devices (Cui 2013, 48). Given the extent of grievances against the state, protests often became violent, thus raising the probability of destabilization (Yan 2013; Wang 2013, 56). This called for a resolute response from the repressive organs.

As we discuss the role of cell phones in protest mobilization, we should keep in mind that they can be a double-edged sword. On the one hand, they facilitate mobilization, as they allow citizens to use social media apps to coordinate their protest activities. Research documents the role of cell phone mobilization in the Hong Kong protests (Jun Liu 2013; Holbig 2020). On the other hand, as revealed by classified police and government yearbooks (Dimitrov 2023), cell phones allow the police to monitor the organization of incipient protests and to either prevent them from taking place or to defuse them during an early stage.

This surveillance capacity explains why police are present at the overwhelming majority of protests and why the incidence of protests declined to a certain extent in the 2010s (Cai and Chen 2022). We should note that when a new technology is introduced, there might be a brief period during which citizens have an advantage vis-à-vis the authorities (as illustrated, for instance by the use of cell phones during the protest mobilization by Falun Gong followers in 1999), but this advantage quickly erodes once the authorities step in and regulate the new technological medium.

Beyond technological change, the second development that helps explain the harsher attitudes toward contention under Xi Jinping is that the number of protests continued to mount under his predecessor, Hu Jintao. Official statistics on this issue became a carefully guarded state secret in 2005, though data have surfaced to indicate that there has been an increase in incidence since 2005 (see Figure 2). Research based on internal documents reveals a twofold rise in the number of protests between 2005 (when they stood at 87,000) and 2013 (when they reached 165,000) (Zhang and Chen 2014). The rising incidence of protests reflected two new realities of the 2000s, which made it difficult to solve problems through the familiar tactic of one-off financial largesse ("buying stability") (Takeuchi 2014). One new development is that grievances were increasingly stemming from transactions between two private parties (e.g., a nonstate-owned firm and its employees), thus limiting government intervention and adjudication. In addition, tolerance for land grabs in rural areas and the illegal demolition of urban housing to make way for lucrative development projects had become widespread as a result of the failure of the central government to adequately fund local governments. Faced with these thorny issues, the party-state opted for a hard-line response. This explains why there is a strong relationship between protests and provincial expenditures on public security in 2014 ($t=9.13$ and r-squared of 0.74 in a bivariate regression in the Dimitrov and Zhang dataset).

Third, there has been increasing insecurity among the top leadership due to the declining popularity of the party-state, as initially reported in an internal publication summarizing the results of the 2013 China Social Survey. This survey detected an erosion in support for the party-state, the courts, and the police (*Lingdao Canyue* 2014). Though these results are at odds with Western (Dickson 2016; Lianjiang Li 2016; Cunningham, Saich, and Turiel 2020) and some Chinese (Li, Chen, and Wang 2020, 128) opinion polling that documents a high level of support for the central government, they are bolstered by other findings in Chinese surveys, where participants express a low level of trust in party and government officials (Li, Chen, and Zhang 2015, 123), a declining belief that voting in grassroots elections has an impact on final electoral outcomes (Li, Chen, and Zhang 2015, 132; Li, Chen, and Zhang 2019, 157), and skepticism that participation in political activities can influence the government (Li, Chen, and Wang 2020, 138). The party-state focuses on such skeptical responses, rather than on the ones indicating support for the central government, and rightly interprets protests as a sign of the lack of trust among the masses (Tian 2012).

The cumulative effect of these three factors was a hard-line response to socioeconomic contention under Xi Jinping, in contrast to the more tolerant approach to protests in the 1990s and 2000s that has been widely theorized in the existing literature. Under Xi, compromise and negotiation have been highly atypical responses to socioeconomic grievances. This is consistent with recent findings about a general repressive turn during the 2010s (Wang and Minzner 2015; Scoggins 2021; Cai and Chen 2022; Ong 2022), about the dire straits of workers who experience "informed disenchantment" with the legal system (and who are thus more likely to join violent protests) (Gallagher 2017), and about the high risk of engaging in visible acts of contention (Fu 2018), especially when directed against the central government (Chen and Cai 2021). Under Xi Jinping, all protests (be they political, socioeconomic, or nationalist) are considered a threat to stability that requires a resolute response. Yet, given that protests index dissatisfaction with government responsiveness, their suppression merely exacerbates discontent. Ultimately, the CCP must find ways to take the citizenry off the streets and to bring them back to the petitioning system, which allows for information to be transmitted privately and thus does not possess the politically destabilizing collective action potential of protests.

3.4 Online Petitioning

The preceding paragraphs have presented evidence of a diminishing responsiveness to both complaints and protests. We might think that the decline in the number of petitions is compensated for by the increased use of online complaints. We should of course stress that the petitioning statistics presented in Figure 1 include complaints submitted by letter, in person, as well as online. The data, compiled by the author by consulting Chinese provincial yearbooks, clearly point out that since 2017 online complaints have become dominant. Nonetheless, the aggregate number of complaints is declining. But what about the various hotlines that have been introduced to allow citizens to contact the government directly? Since 2018 provinces have created so-called "12345" portals, with the goal of allowing citizens to register all problems by visiting a single website (*yiwang tongban*) or by making a single phone call to the 12345 number (Qinghai 2019, 110). Could it be that individuals are using these portals instead of the formal complaints system? Here we must distinguish between the functions of the portals and the functions of the complaint system. The portals are the latest incarnation of government hotlines, which were transformed into "ask the mayor" websites in the 2000s (Distelhorst and Hou 2017). Both the old hotlines and the new portals are overwhelmingly focused on providing factual information about government services. Occasionally, citizens may contact government offices simply to vent or to chat (Ding 2020; 2022). By contrast, complaints are grievances stemming from some type of violation of the law, such as illegal land taking, forcible destruction of housing, or nonpayment of wages or welfare benefits. Although often conflated in the English-language literature on Chinese politics, requests for information are different from complaints. This explains why the number of complaints has declined, even as requests for information have increased. That being said, we should take seriously the ambition of the party to eventually make the 12345 portals into digital equivalents of letters and visits offices. Future research may be able to demonstrate whether over time the 12345 portals are beginning to handle more matters resembling the grievances received by the *xinfang* offices.

How effective are these portals in contacting the authorities, when compared with the complaints system? Data from Hunan province allow us to answer this question. Its "Internet and supervision WeChat platform" ("*hulianwang+jiancha*" *pingtai*) received 1.2 billion WeChat text messages in 2019 denouncing corruption, with some especially zealous users submitting over 95,000 messages (Hunan 2020, 135–136). However, most of this information was simply noise. For instance, the 1.2 billion messages led to the disciplining of only 619 individuals and the transfer of only five individuals to the judicial authorities (Hunan 2020, 135–136). Contrast this with the corruption denunciations received through the standard CCP Discipline Inspection channels: in Hunan, there were 72,224 such corruption denunciations in 2019, which resulted in the disciplining of 19,603 party members (Hunan 2020, 136). This is twenty-five times more than the number of individuals disciplined as a result of corruption denunciations submitted via the WeChat platform. In sum, though numerous, WeChat platform messages are much less effective than complaints submitted in person or online through the regular corruption denunciation and petitioning mechanisms operated by the communist party and the government.

3.5 Conclusion: Declining Responsiveness to Welfare Demands

The market social contract contains certain pitfalls for the regime. Under the socialist social contract in Eastern Europe, citizens expected a steady increase in the standard of living as a result of economic growth and extensive price subsidies. In addition, they received a comprehensive package of welfare benefits (lifetime employment, subsidized housing, free healthcare and education, and universal pensions at age fifty-five for women and age sixty for men); important-ly, inequality was low. In China under Mao, the socialist social contract extended only to a subset of the urban population. The market social contract currently in place involves elevated levels of economic growth, universal pensions (at age fifty or age fifty-five for women and age sixty for men, to be gradually extended to fifty-five or fifty-eight for women and sixty-three for men by the end of 2039), health insurance, and access to free education through junior high school. Apart from the extreme inequalities in wealth and the vast regional and sectoral disparities in welfare provision, discontent is high because of difficulties enforcing labor regulations, insecurity of urban property rights (especially over housing), and displacement of rural residents from their homes due to lucrative land redevelopment schemes supported by local governments. Trust in the party in the 2010s was declining and it presumably decreased even further during the initial cover-up of COVID-19 and during the 2022 lockdowns. It is unclear how much longer the party-state will be able to direct welfare discontent away from Beijing to the local governments. Should dissatisfaction turn against the central government, systemwide instability is likely to follow. Therefore, it is imperative for the party-state to ensure that there is high responsiveness to popular grievances.

4 Protecting Cultural Security and Promoting Indigenous Cultural Consumption

Autocracies are apprehensive about their relations with foreign powers, which may pose potential economic, military, or political threats. Western ideological influence, in particular, can create a political hazard in dictatorships. This section is concerned with the responses that China has deployed to such threats. The argument presented here highlights the rise of a dual strategy, which includes hard defensive measures of protecting cultural security but also draws on a soft offensive tool kit centered around promoting indigenous cultural consumption. These policies have different goals: on the one hand to prevent access to ideologically subversive materials and on the other to distract citizens from searching for such content. Although both the hard defensive and the soft offensive approaches emerged prior to 1989, it was the Tiananmen protests and the collapse of communism in Europe that consolidated understandings of cultural security and indigenous cultural consumption as the two dominant strategies for countering ideological threats to regime resilience after the end of the Cold War. The guiding philosophy has been that one of the key reasons for the Soviet collapse was lax political and ideological protection (Zongti Guojia Anquan Guan 2016, 80).

Before we proceed, we should note that Chinese conceptions of culture are broad, thus producing an expansive view of the range of cultural security threats and of the availability of counteroffensive strategies. According to the Xinhua dictionary, culture is "the sum of material and spiritual wealth created by human beings in the process of their social and historical development, especially spiritual wealth like philosophy, technology, education, literature, the arts, etc." (Xinhua 2004, 504). This broad conceptualization of culture leads to considering everything from European languages to Japanese anime and block-chain technology as cultural security threats (Jiang 2016; Liu Yanping 2013; Yao and Wu 2021) and to regarding Huawei products, the Chinese language, Chinese food, and traditional Chinese medicine as counteroffensive weapons in the struggle to build cultural soft power (Tao and Yin 2021; He, Tian, and Song 2020). Culture is indeed a broad concept in China.

The section is divided into five parts. It begins by reviewing the main avenues for spreading ideological influence and by placing China's respective responses to such threats in comparative perspective. The second part provides a chronological investigation of cultural security, culminating in its inclusion into the concept of comprehensive national security under Xi Jinping. We should not be mistaken about the political implications, as Xi stated in 2013 that "regime collapse often starts in the ideological sphere" (Guojia Wenhua Anquan 2022, 8–9). The narrative in this part focuses on the Ministry of Public Security (MPS) and the Ministry of State Security (MSS), which are the two key bureaucracies tasked with protecting cultural security. This part also highlights the techniques that the two ministries used to blunt the main vectors for propagating political, ethnic minority, and religious threats to cultural security. The third part focuses on the soft strategies of indigenous cultural consumption. The cultural products promoted by the CCP range from pure entertainment at one extreme to pure propaganda on the other. The immediate goal is to distract from searching for Western cultural products. A longer-term aspiration is to render hostile foreign ideology useless through the building of patriotic pride. The fourth part focuses on the response to external ideological influence during COVID-19. The final part assesses the limited success of the CCP's soft strategies and concludes the section by reviewing the return to strict censorship during Xi Jinping's second term in office.

4.1 The War of Ideas

Ideology formed a fundamental part of the rivalry between democracy and autocracy both during and after the Cold War. As early as 1950, the US National Security Council (NSC) prepared a brief for President Truman that outlined the "basic conflict between the idea of freedom … and the idea of slavery"

(NSC 68, 7). Although the classified memo presents several options for dealing with the communist threat, it concludes that the most effective course of action involves overt political and psychological warfare aimed at encouraging anti-government unrest (NSC 68, 57). Thus began the fight for hearts and minds, which was waged on the cultural front. This means that Western cultural products, such as literature, film, music, fashion, and radio and TV programs, came to serve as carriers of the ideas of freedom. It is no coincidence that Francis Fukuyama encapsulates his wildly optimistic views about the triumph of the Western idea as "the ultimate victory of the VCR" (Fukuyama 1992, 108), or "liberal democracy in the political sphere combined with easy access to VCRs and stereos in the economic" (Fukuyama 1989, 8).

To understand why, with the benefit of hindsight, Fukuyama's end of history appears to have been a myth, we need to analyze the defensive and offensive countermeasures deployed by all communist autocracies to blunt the force of Western ideology. Contrasting China with Eastern Europe provides further insights into why the triumph of democracy and the end of history ultimately proved partial at best.

4.1.1 Countermeasures to Blunt Western Ideological Influence

All communist regimes deploy a combination of hard defensive and soft offensive measures in response to liberal ideas. The defensive measures identify the avenues for the spread of ideas and then aim to neutralize them. In addition to news content, these vectors include literary and artistic works like film and music. They are transmitted through different media platforms that traditionally included books, newsprint, records, cassette tapes, and electronic broadcasts, but since the 1980s, the media spectrum has been expanded by the addition of VHS tapes, CDs, DVDs, the Internet, and eventually social media. Traditionally, nonbroadcast media circulated with the assistance of tourists, students, businesspeople, diplomats, journalists, artists, and performers, who carried and transmitted them; the Internet has made circulation largely independent of such human couriers. Thus, whereas in the pre-digital age the focus of the secret police was on jamming broadcasts and stopping the illegal circulation of offensive media content brought in by human couriers, the advent of the Internet has resulted in censorship efforts being directed nearly exclusively toward blocking legal imports and preventing the circulation of digital media.

Beyond deploying hard defensive measures to prevent ideological subversion and to safeguard cultural security, communist states also mount a soft ideological counteroffensive that involves the promotion of indigenous (Chinese) cultural production and consumption. The primary audience for this counteroffensive is domestic, and the aim is twofold. First, by providing high-quality indigenous content, the regime can dissuade citizens from searching for apolitical foreign entertainment and accidentally finding potentially subversive material. This strategy of distraction was employed in the analog era in Eastern Europe and has been adapted to the Internet age in China (Dimitrov 2023; Roberts 2018); it also parallels the recent regime efforts in Saudi Arabia to create an alternative to external cultural influences (Alsudairi 2019). A second aim of domestic cultural production is to build national pride. Grandiose spectacles like the hosting of the Olympics help generate feelings of patriotism that are continuously reinforced by the powerful communist party propaganda system, which dictates all domestic media content. We should note that the cultural offensive is also aimed at a secondary external audience, with the goal of projecting soft power and generating positive feelings toward the regime among foreign citizens. This occurred both in the Eastern Bloc prior to 1989 and in contemporary China (Dragostinova 2021; Barmé 2009; Repnikova 2022).

4.1.2 Chinese Vulnerability to Ideological Influence in Comparative Perspective

Comparative analysis reveals that vulnerability to the Western ideological threat has varied over both time and space in the communist universe. Chinese exposure to Western ideological influence never rose to Eastern European levels. When Western media penetration peaked in 2018, the audience for US media reached 6.2 percent of the adult population in China, up from 0.3 percent in 2015 (US Agency for Global Media 2018, 15). By contrast, the average share of the adult population that listened to Western radio consistently exceeded 50 percent during the Cold War in several Eastern European countries (Hoover Institution 2004, 45–47). Perhaps the most consequential difference between Eastern Europe and China is that the 1975 Helsinki Final Act bound the European communist regimes to a treaty that facilitated the free movement of ideas and people (Thomas 2001), thus ultimately making it impossible to effectively counteract Western influence through the promotion of indigenous cultural production and consumption. No similar constraint has yet emerged in China, despite significant outbound tourism and overseas work and study. This has enabled the regime to maximize its reliance on defensive and offensive strategies aimed at safeguarding cultural security.

4.2 Hard Defense: Protecting Cultural Security

Since the 1950s, cultural protection has provided a broad umbrella for deploying defensive tactics against ideological infiltration. After defining the concept and describing its evolution over time, we move to a discussion of the functions of the two main entities tasked with safeguarding cultural security – the MPS and the MSS. We conclude by elaborating on the specific techniques deployed by the two ministries against the main threats to cultural security.

4.2.1 Continuity and Change in Cultural Protection

Emerging in the 1950s, concerns about cultural protection intensified in the 1980s and became especially pronounced after the dissolution of the Soviet Union, when internal government documents identify "hostile overseas forces" (*jingwai didui shili*) as responsible for promoting the strategy of peaceful evolution toward democracy (Guojia Anquan Bu 1990b; Guojia Anquan Bu 1991). Although historically Taiwan and the Soviet Union had been China's main ideological adversaries, the West assumed that position after 1989. China's entry into the WTO in 2001 exacerbated preexisting fears about the impact of external forces on domestic stability and intensified the ongoing process of securitizing cultural threats (Fürst 2021). The Color Revolutions in the 2000s and Arab Spring in the early 2010s further sensitized the leadership to the ongoing threat of subversion.

Therefore, responding to the West became imperative in the 2010s. The 2013 Document No. 9 resolutely opposes the infiltration of Western values by specifying the "seven don't mentions" (*qi bu jiang*) of constitutional democracy; universal human rights; civil society; freedom of the press; neoliberalism; historical nihilism; and questioning the socialist orientation of the post-1978 reforms. These issues remain off-limits for any media discussion in China. In 2014, cultural security was included in Xi Jinping's definition of comprehensive state security (*zongti guojia anquan guan*) (Xi 2014). Guarding against and resisting negative cultural influences is explicitly discussed in Article 23 of the 2015 National Security Law. Currently, the concept is firmly integrated into Chinese notions of comprehensive state (national) security. Importantly, cultural security is used interchangeably with ideological security (*yishixingtai anquan*) and political security (*zhengzhi anquan*) (Han 2016; Johnson 2017; Alsudairi 2019; Yan and Alsudairi 2021; Guojia Wenhua Anquan 2022). This speaks to the capaciousness of the concept. Safeguarding something as far-ranging as cultural security requires substantial bureaucratic resources.

4.2.2 Protecting Cultural Security: The Ministry of Public Security and the Ministry of State Security

From the establishment of the PRC in 1949 until the creation of the MSS in 1983, the MPS had exclusive jurisdiction over implementation of the defensive measures to protect cultural security. The MSS was established in response to the elevated threat of ideological subversion during the initial post-Mao reform period, when foreign investment was bringing both capital and new ideas into the country (Guojia Anquan Bu 1987; Guoji Guanxi Xueyuan 2010, 32). MSS work summaries indicate that both before and after 1989 the Ministry has strived to counteract infiltration attempts by hostile foreign forces (Guojia Anquan Bu 1987; 1989; 1990a; 1990b; 1991).

During the four decades since the creation of the MSS, the MPS has continued to engage in cultural protection work, which is understood to be a key component of political security protection and therefore of the MPS state security protection portfolio (Beijing Shi Gong'an Ju 2001; 2014). MPS cultural protection includes tracking foreign NGOs and their activities, identifying politically subversive publications, monitoring religious and cult activities, maintaining control over political stability in universities and research institutes, and surveilling the Internet for harmful content (Beijing Shi 2020; Zhejiang Gong'an 2021). In sum, both the MSS and the MPS see ideological infiltration as the root cause of the domestic state security problems that run the gamut from human rights to minority unrest. The broad scope of cultural security makes it a useful lens into Chinese understandings of how external forces impact domestic political processes.

4.2.3 Hostile Foreign Forces as a Threat to Cultural Security

Internal government documents leave no doubt that hostile foreign forces are regarded as a threat to cultural security because of the subversive ideas they can transmit. Here we will discuss this ideological influence in three specific spheres (political, ethnic minority, and religious) and will outline the concrete responses by the MSS and the MPS.

Political ideas can be threatening. One example is the notion of "peaceful evolution," a strategy to subvert socialism from within – through economic, cultural, and political means, such as trade, promotion of Western lifestyles, and pressure to protect human rights (Guojia Anquan Bu 1991; *Neibu Canyue* 1991). Another example is the democracy movement, which has included famous dissidents like Liu Xiaobo and exiles like Teng Biao. A third is rights defense (*weiquan*), a movement of lawyers and intellectuals that arose in the 2000s with the aim to protect civil rights through litigation (*Renmin Xinfang* 2010, 6). According to the CCP, hostile forces are the central external actor working to destabilize China. They are identified as the motor behind the three evil forces (*sangu shili*) of terrorism, separatism, and religious extremism in Xinjiang (*Renmin Ribao* 2013). Similarly, in Tibet, the Dalai Lama is seen as a hostile foreign influence promoting independence (Qin 1990, 1–59; Renzhen Luose et al. 2001, 1). Finally, turning to religious proselytizing, both subversive faiths (Islam, Tibetan Buddhism, and the quasi-religious practice of Falun Gong) and mainstream Catholic and Protestant fellowship are perceived as vectors for foreign infiltration and thus as a threat to cultural security (Xu et al. 2016; Han 2016).

This raises the question of countermeasures. It is well known that China has an extensive censorship apparatus that relies on fear, friction (creating barriers for those who want to access some type of information), and flooding (whereby users are distracted by entertaining content that makes it less likely that they will look for objectionable material) (Roberts 2018). Censorship extends to both legacy media and to content that is transmitted through the Internet. With regard to legacy media, censorship encompasses print media (newspapers and magazines), electronic media (radio and TV), books, film and music (both live performances and screenings, as well as works encoded on tapes, CDs, and DVDs), and computer games. All such content produced or imported into China must be officially approved by the CCP Propaganda Department and its affiliated bureaucracies in charge of copyright administration, press and publications, and culture. Although prohibited media content circulates as a byproduct of piracy (Mertha 2005; Dimitrov 2009), the rates of piracy of legacy media have declined in recent years, reflecting both increased enforcement and moves to online media consumption (Dimitrov 2016).

As most media consumption began to shift to the Internet in the 2000s, efforts to censor content changed correspondingly. Today, a vast apparatus of entities is tasked with weeding out inappropriate content. Front and center is the CCP Propaganda (Publicity) Department, whose government equivalent is the State Council Information Office. This practice of corresponding party and government offices is known as "one organization, two nameplates." It ensures that the party has direct control over the public-facing departments handling extremely sensitive tasks such as censorship. Beneath the CCP Propaganda Department sits the Central Cybersecurity and Informatization Commission, whose public-facing name is the Cyberspace Administration of China. According to the principle of "one organization, two nameplates," Zhuang Rongwen heads both cyberspace entities, while also concurrently serving as vice director of the Propaganda Department. The cybersecurity divisions of the Propaganda Department conduct their own monitoring and assessments of websites and social media accounts and issue binding censorship instructions to Internet service providers (Gansu 2020, 60–61; Hubei 2020, 47–48; also see Miller 2018). In addition to the Propaganda Department, the MPS is also actively engaged in overseeing the Internet and social media conglomerates, deleting objectionable material and punishing those who generate, transmit, or consume it (Beijing Shi Gong'an Ju 2014, 155; Beijing Shi 2020, 382–385; Guangdong 2021, 106).

Although there is agreement that censorship is pervasive, there is no consensus on what Internet content is more likely to be targeted for deletion. An influential article argues that Internet posts that simply criticize the government will not be deleted, unless they also have a potential for collective action (King, Pan, and Roberts 2013). Even though the collective action part of the argument makes sense, some scholars point out that only solicited critical feedback (in the period leading up to the passage of a new law or regulation, for instance) is allowed to survive; unsolicited criticism is deleted (Gueorguiev and Malesky 2019). Other experts, studying censorship instructions, have similarly taken issue with the argument in King, Pan, and Roberts (2013) that unprompted criticism of the government can survive on the Chinese Internet (Miller 2018). There is also research stressing that it matters who posts rather than what is posted – posts by individuals with many followers (the so-called Big Vs) are more likely to be deleted because the Propaganda Department is concerned about their viral potential (Gallagher and Miller 2021). These debates highlight that reaching scholarly consensus on an issue as complex as the scope and guiding principles of Internet censorship in China may not be possible given the powerful incentives for the CCP to maintain secrecy about sensitive activities such as information control.

Beyond censorship, another countermeasure aimed at hostile foreign forces is the deployment of onerous MPS registration rules that make it more difficult for foreign NGOs to operate in China and for Chinese NGOs to receive foreign funding (Holbig and Lang 2022). This appears to be working, as only 605 foreign NGOs have maintained their registration since the Overseas NGO Law entered into force in 2017 (as opposed to 7,000 foreign NGOs operating prior to 2017) – and most of them focus on relatively noncontroversial issues like the promotion of industry and trade or the provision of educational services (China NGO Project 2022). Gone are the days when international civil-society organizations in China could work on human rights. Fundamentally, the guiding principle for managing hostile foreign forces is that ideas can be controlled by monitoring foreigners, who are seen as likely vectors for their propagation (Yu 1990, 127–142; Han 2016). Cartoons found on Chinese street displays aim to sensitize citizens to the danger that foreign spies are posing as tourists or students (or, alternatively, are pretending to be in love with Chinese women in order to extract state secrets). To exercise control over hostile foreign forces, the MPS and MSS draw on informants and promote citizen denunciations. In 2023, for instance, the reward for turning in foreign spies was set as high as RMB500,000 (about US$70,000) (*The Economist* 2023).

With regard to religious threats, a variegated and dynamic response has been developed. From 1989 to the mid-2010s, severe repression of some religions was combined with relative tolerance of others. Tibetan Buddhism was approached with distrust, which increased following the 2008 Lhasa protests (Xue et al. 2016, 164–165). For this reason, the long-term decline in the number of Buddhist monks and nuns, from 8.6 percent of the population of Tibet in 1958 (Dimitrov 2023, 261) to 1.3 percent in 2019 (Xizang 2021, 370) was a welcome development for the central authorities in Beijing. Hostility extended to Islam, which is regarded as a vector of extremism in Xinjiang, especially after 9/11 (Guowuyuan Fazhan Yanjiu Zhongxin 2004; Alsudairi 2019). The all-out attack on Islamic faith and practice intensified in the 2010s and culminated in the creation of massive reeducation camps for the Uyghurs in Xinjiang. Threat perceptions also include Falun Gong, whose practitioners have been persecuted, as documented in the English-language literature (Palmer 2007; Tong 2009) and in Chinese police gazetteers. At the same time, the attitude toward Christian denominations is somewhat different. One scholar finds evidence of collaboration between the state and religious communities (Koesel 2014). Another shows that protestant churches possess more autonomy from the party than is usually assumed (Vala 2017). Similarly, one political scientist argues that the MPS subjects unregistered small-scale Protestant house churches to infiltration and surveillance but not to outright crackdowns (Reny 2018). We can make sense of these findings by keeping in mind that they are based on research conducted prior to the mid-2010s, when Christians, in contrast to Falun Gong practitioners, Muslims, and Tibetan Buddhists, were typically not perceived to be subversive. This changed after Xi Jinping assumed office.

The main doctrinal innovation under Xi Jinping has been the Sinification (*zhongguohua*) of religion. The concept of Sinification grew out of scholarly discussions of religion with Chinese socialist characteristics (*Zhongguo tese shehui zhuyi zongjiao*). This theoretical debate aimed to clarify a crucial point that is treated relatively vaguely in Document No. 19 of 1982 that outlines the CCP's views on religion – namely, the specific role of the party in managing religious organizations. At first glance, treatises about religion with Chinese socialist characteristics are dry extrapolations of how Marxism can be reconciled with religion. Yet, occasionally, these academic writings reveal what is truly at stake for the CCP. One such piece provides major insights into the threefold problem that the party faces from organized religion: separation of church and state (*zhengjiao fenli*) means that religious organizations may oppose the party and threaten state security; the foreign links of organized religion present a channel for infiltration; and the absence of firm party control over religion threatens the patriotic national unity of all ethnic groups (Zhu 2005). Those problems necessitated a turn to Sinification, which some scholars have called the "partification" (*danghua*) of religion (Jing and Koesel 2024).

Views on the Sinification of religion were developed between 2013 and 2017 in a series of meetings, which culminated in five-year plans for the Sinification of all major religions in China as well as policy guidance for the management of religious groups. These documents outline both doctrinal and administrative changes that leave no ambiguity about the CCP's ambition to assert control over religious expression. On the doctrinal front, Sinification aims to align religious practice with the goals of the party; for example, it involves replacing original scriptural texts with excerpts and summaries that support the Core Socialist Values (prosperity, democracy, civility, and harmony; freedom, equality, justice, and the rule of law; patriotism, dedication, integrity, and friendship) (*Five-Year Planning Outline for Advancing the Sinification of Christianity* 2017). In addition, decisions of party congresses are to be discussed during religious services. To summarize, the Chinese character of all religions is to be emphasized and foreign influence is to be eliminated (*Five-Year Planning Outline for Persisting in the Sinification of Islam* 2017). Regulations in 2024 mandating that mosque architecture in Xinjiang "reflect Chinese characteristics and style" provide a recent highly visible example of Sinification (Wong 2024). Administratively, all religious organizations are subject to strict formal registration rules. Finally, the *Measures for the Administration of Religious Groups* (2019) leave no doubt that any thought of religious independence from the party-state should be abandoned. In sum, unsupervised organized religion is seen as an ideological threat to state security.

4.3 Soft Counteroffensive Measures

Along with the hard defensive policies outlined thus far, softer strategies like patriotic education, traditional learning (*guoxue*), resisting linguistic hegemony, and promoting indigenous cultural production have been deployed as techniques to counteract Western ideological infiltration by building cultural confidence (*wenhua zixin*) and national pride.[4] In contrast to the defensive measures, which are the prerogative of the MPS and MSS, the counteroffensive strategies are deployed by the powerful CCP Propaganda Department, which oversees all bureaucracies in charge of culture, print and publications, and education. The Propaganda Department decides on crucial doctrinal matters like the ideological content of cultural products that are allowed to circulate through analog

---

[4] www.xinhuanet.com/politics/xxjxs/2019-06/19/c_1124642114.htm.

and digital means. It also sanctions the production of ideological entertainment like the 2023 Hunan TV five-part series *When Marx Met Confucius*, which aims to popularize a key element in Xi Jinping's Thoughts on Culture, namely the possibility of combining Marxism with Confucianism.[5]

4.3.1 Patriotic Education and Traditional Learning

Though it emerged in the 1980s as part of the campaign against bourgeois liberalization, patriotic education persists to the current day. Students at all levels are exposed to a curriculum that stresses history, politics, and ideology. Elementary schools teach a compulsory subject called "Xi Jinping Thought on Socialism with Chinese Characteristics for the New Era." University entrance exams feature political questions (Koesel 2020; Howlett 2021) and university students are subjected to a heavy ideological curriculum (Yan 2014; Perry 2020), which is explicitly conceptualized as a countermeasure to blunt Western attempts at infiltration (Li Yingjun 2016). Significant attention is also paid to the ideological impact of the Internet on college students (Lu 2020). The results are consistent with the CCP's intended goals: an experimental study reveals that higher levels of trust for government officials and distrust of Western-style democracy among Peking University students are associated with exposure to the more ideological high-school politics curriculum introduced in 2004–10 (Cantoni et al. 2017). Patriotic education seems to be delivering what the party wants.

A related strategy is the promotion of traditional learning/national learning (*guoxue*), which in the Chinese-language literature is used interchangeably with terms like China studies (*Zhongguo xue*) or Sinology (*hanxue*). Although the history of the concept of traditional learning goes back at least to the *ti–yong* debates of the Self-Strengthening Movement at the end of the Qing dynasty (*zhongxue wei ti, xixue wei yong* – Chinese learning for the essence, Western learning for application), its contemporary relevance is a result of the culture fever (*wenhua re*) of the 1980s (Li 2008). In the 1990s and the 2000s, a number of universities established national learning research institutes, and undergraduate political education curricula were reorganized to include more content on Chinese classics, history, and philosophy (Wang 2009; Ding and Rao 2021). Scholars began to write about a "national learning fever" (*guoxue re*) (Li 2007; Wang 2009; Liu 2020). The CCP promoted traditional learning as an antidote to Western culture. The ultimate goal was to foster cultural awareness and build national cultural identity (*minzu wenhua rentong*) (Zhao 2004; Li 2007), at least among the Han Chinese – it remains unclear how restive minorities such as the Tibetans and the Uyghurs embrace concepts like *guoxue* and patriotic education.

---

[5] www.youtube.com/watch?v=Fyv4iwlt604.

4.3.2 Resisting Linguistic Hegemony

Foreign ideas are transmitted through language. The study of English in particular, which has been widespread in China, has presented a potential vector for cultural infiltration should a sufficient number of citizens master it to a high level. Therefore, the party-state maintains that safeguarding cultural security requires counteracting the linguistic hegemony (*yuyan baquan*) that reflects the global cultural dominance of English (Yang and Zhang 2010). A more recent argument focuses on the economic gains associated with the global dominance of English (Lu and Zhou 2020). Resisting linguistic hegemony involves the steps taken in the 2010s to reduce the weighting of the English component of the university entrance exams (*gaokao*) and to encourage students to be tested in languages other than English. Attention to the effects of promoting English through online interactions (chat rooms, gaming, texting) is also visible (Chen 2013). Other measures to oppose Western cultural hegemony (*xifang wenhua baquan*) center around elevating the status of Mandarin (rather than any of the other languages spoken in China, such as Cantonese, Uyghur, Mongolian, or Tibetan) by increasing Chinese-language content on the Internet and sponsoring the establishment of Confucius Institutes around the world (Li 2007). With more Mandarin speakers, both traditional Confucian culture and ideological tropes like Chinese conceptions of democracy can be successfully promoted (Zhang 2012). Relatedly, retrospective accounts point out that the insufficient state backing of the Russian language was one of the reasons for the Soviet collapse (He and Hu 2022). In sum, the CCP is fully cognizant of the soft power associated with language and therefore it seeks to dislodge English from its global leadership position. However, the recent closure of nearly all the Confucius Institutes in the United States and in other Western countries raises doubts about the long-term success of this strategy.

4.3.3 Promoting Indigenous Cultural Production

Limiting the impact of Western culture requires not only blocking or regulating access but, equally important, developing indigenous cultural products that can replace imports or at least distract citizens from the desire to consume them (Zhang 2012; Han 2016). Ultimately, the goal is to raise the profile of domestic cultural products and to build cultural soft power, for example, by developing the film or music industry.

Import bans and quotas are imposed both to filter offensive content and to promote the domestic cultural industry. For instance, Chinese censors allow no more than thirty-four foreign films to be screened for box office receipts every year, thus creating less competition for domestic feature films. These efforts have been successful, as the share of non-Chinese films viewed in movie theaters consistently declined during the 2010s, from a high of 55 percent in 2012 to a low of 12 percent in 2021 (Xiao and Chen 2022) (Chinese films accounted for 84.49 percent of box office sales in 2021 [Guojia Wenhua Anquan 2022, 101–102]). Official plans for development of the film industry call on it to promote Chinese values, Chinese esthetics, the Chinese language, and Chinese power throughout the world (Guojia Wenhua Anquan 2022, 101). Thus, domestically the film industry is tasked with contributing to the building of cultural self-confidence, while internationally it is meant to project cultural soft power. Similar domestic and international logics drive official support for cultural heritage tourism sites, parks, and monuments (Guojia Wenhua Anquan 2022, 65–73).

One aspect of the promotion of indigenous culture is the enthusiasm for national brands (*guochao*) like Huawei, Xiaomi, Huili, Anta, and China Lining (Wang Xing 2021). Consumption of these "China-chic" products is seen both as an expression of patriotism and as a way to oppose Western cultural infiltration. These Chinese brands are understood to be strong competitors to Japanese and Korean fashions, which are subject to criticism that is similar to that of Western products. Furthermore, the growing appeal of national brands overseas also contributes to the building of cultural soft power. For example, the popularity of TikTok shows that foreign consumers are willing to embrace Chinese technology.

4.3.4 Fostering National Pride, Promoting Cultural Confidence, and Building Soft Power

In late 2012 and throughout 2013, Xi Jinping made a series of statements about the Chinese dream of the great rejuvenation of the Chinese nation. Initially, these concepts were somewhat vague, but a March 2014 speech clarifies Xi's vision that culture is essential for realizing the Chinese dream. Xi argues that China had cultural pride (*wenhua zihaogan*) prior to the Opium Wars, but the ensuing century of national humiliation greatly diminished its cultural confidence (*wenhua zixin*). The Chinese dream therefore is a dream of national cultural rejuvenation (Qi 2016). These arguments are built on earlier investigations into how cultural awareness (*wenhua zijue*) can foster national pride through grandiose spectacles, such as the hosting of the 2008 Summer Olympics (Yun 2010). More recent efforts to highlight cultural confidence focus on ice and snow sports and the hosting of the 2022 Winter Olympics (Wang et al. 2020). Ultimately, the goal is to build cultural soft power (Yun 2010; Pan and Liu 2016), as is appropriate for any country that has reemerged as a great power.

4.4 Fears of a Color Revolution under COVID-19: Hostile Foreign Forces in the 2020s

New challenges continue to be seen through the familiar lens of hostile foreign forces meddling in Chinese domestic affairs and fomenting a color revolution. The term "color revolutions" is typically used to describe the demise of autocracies in the 1990s and the 2000s, primarily in Eastern Europe and the former Soviet Union. Those electoral revolutions involved dislodging postcommunist leaders through the ballot box (Bunce and Wolchik 2011). Despite the absence of electoral politics in China, the leadership is worried about contagion because the color revolutions also involved extensive anti-regime mobilization (Koesel and Bunce 2013). Such fears were exacerbated in the 2000s, with China experiencing hundreds of thousands of protests per year that were regarded as threats to social and political stability, as noted in Section 3. The popular mobilization that characterized Arab Spring (even if the electoral dimension was largely absent) led to similar concerns about contagion of anti-regime contention. Hong Kong, which has the status of a Special Administrative Region (SAR), was also rocked by ongoing anti-government protests throughout the 2010s. Finally, the anti-war protests that erupted throughout Russia in the spring of 2022, following Putin's invasion of Ukraine, were similarly viewed by the Chinese authorities as the beginning of an incipient color revolution, whose spillover potential to China must be blocked (Introvigne 2022). The common denominator in Chinese thinking about the color revolutions, Arab Spring, the Hong Kong protests, and the anti-war movement in Russia is that they all were instigated by hostile foreign forces – and that China must remain vigilant about the influence of such external factors.

Concern about hostile foreign forces persisted throughout the COVID-19 pandemic. After nearly three years of periodic lockdowns and numerous other restrictions guided by the goal of minimizing COVID-19 infections, protests emerged in dozens of Chinese cities in November 2022. As the participants were not allowed to raise banners with slogans or comments, they held up sheets of A4 paper that were simply blank (these events are now -commonly referred to as the White Paper Protests or the A4 Revolution). Although the zero-COVID policies were ultimately repealed, the highest-profile protest organizers were detained. These contentious episodes were portrayed as being instigated by hostile foreign forces (*jingwai fanhua shili*) by wolf-warrior diplomat Lu Shaye, China's ambassador to France (Deutsche Welle 2022; see also Martin 2021 on wolf-warrior diplomacy). Ambassador Lu has argued that "white is also a color" and that hostile foreign forces were seeking to bring about a color revolution in China. General Secretary Xi Jinping similarly has highlighted the danger of a color revolution spreading to China. These concerns are reflected in a security threat assessment produced by the Central Political and Legal Affairs Commission in March 2022 (Introvigne 2022). Unsurprisingly, fears of the presumed nexus between hostile foreign forces and public protests that may be transformed into color revolutions persisted during the pandemic.

4.5 The Hard Turn in Cultural Security under Xi

This section analyzes the hard defensive and the soft counteroffensive measures deployed by the CCP in response to the perceived ideological assault on cultural security by hostile foreign forces. In the 2010s, an overall repressive turn was detected in Chinese politics (Wang and Minzner 2015; Gallagher 2017). This also had implications for cultural security. As reaffirmed by Xi Jinping in his July 1, 2021, centenary speech, the party is committed to resisting Western influence. Audiences were reminded that China had withstood "subversion, sabotage, and armed provocation" and it would not allow foreign forces to "bully, oppress, and subjugate" it.[6] Xi is firmly committed to avoiding the fate of the Soviet Union.

The hard turn allows us to make sense of a number of measures, like the crackdown on labor and other rights-based NGOs; the ban on social media publishing any news reports that are not sourced from the official media (thus effectively outlawing citizen journalism); and the general escalation of Internet restrictions after Xi assumed power in 2012–13. These measures are consistent with the blocking of the potential vectors for ideological infiltration and subversion. But what about limiting the amount of time children spend playing computer games; banning foreign educational business; and declaring androgynous stars such as Zhu Zhengting and Liu Yu off-limits on Chinese TV? Or what about Article 34 of the 2023 draft revisions of the Public Security Administration Punishments Law, which allows the police to impose fines or to detain those who negate the deeds of national heroes and martyrs, engage in speech detrimental to the spirit of the Chinese people, or wear clothing that hurts the feelings of the Chinese people? Though they may appear irrational, these restrictions are fully consistent with the goal of protecting cultural security. Their long-term viability will be revisited in the Conclusion to this Element.

5 Rival Incorporation into the Chinese Communist Party

The most serious governance challenge facing any communist regime is the rise of alternative political movements that might disrupt the party-state's monopoly

---

[6] www.xinhuanet.com/2021-07/01/c_1127615334.htm.

on power. This lesson was vigorously reinforced after the collapse of communist regimes in Eastern Europe and Mongolia in 1989–91 due to their long-term economic and ideological decay as well as, ultimately, due to the rise of civil-society groups that were rapidly transformed into proto-opposition parties. As this section argues, the most effective strategy to prevent the emergence of alternative centers of political power in autocracies is the incorporation (co-optation) of potential rivals into the governing institutions of the regime. In a single-party system like China, the key mechanism for implementing rival incorporation is the communist party itself. Since the Tiananmen protests, the CCP continuously broadened its membership base and skillfully co-opted representatives from a wide range of social groups. This is consistent with Huntington's classic argument that a sign of adaptation is that the party is "capable of assimilating the new social forces produced through modernization" (Huntington 1968, 420–421). The ongoing success of these efforts is essential to maintain the stability of single-party rule.

Yet, there is also a trade-off between the rapid expansion in size and the quality of the party. This thinking is revealed in a series of discussions undertaken by the Politburo in the wake of the 2012 Party Congress that culminated in a 2014 decision of the CCP General Office to restrict the quantity and improve the quality of party members. Additional regulations by the Organization Department have introduced stricter rules for admission into the party and have reduced the quota for new party members, except in certain categories such as manufacturing workers, young rural residents, highly educated groups, private entrepreneurs, and NGO staff (Zhonggong Zhongyang Zuzhi Bu 2021b, 525–526). During the past decade, these policies did slow down party growth, but they also led to a drop in applications for membership (which has implications for successful rival incorporation) and to a reduction in the number of party branches in private firms and NGOs (which may restrict the capacity of the CCP to maintain a panoptical vision).

This section will first discuss the general theoretical literature on rival incorporation and the specific functions of the communist party in that respect. We will then focus on the expansion in the size of the party after 1989 and will highlight problems in the systematic penetration of private firms and NGOs that may present challenges to CCP rule. We will subsequently turn to some groups that have proven resistant to incorporation, such as ethnic minorities; residents of Hong Kong and Macau; and intellectuals who are critical of the system. As CCP membership is not the only vehicle to neutralize rivals, we will also examine the United Front system and organizations like the All-China Women's Federation and the All-China Federation of Trade Unions. At the end of the section, we will evaluate the overall success of rival incorporation strategies and will highlight some challenges that may impact the future success of the CCP in maintaining single-party rule.

5.1 Institutions for Rival Incorporation

The general theoretical literature on autocracies investigates the deployment of power-sharing mechanisms, such as cabinet appointments or the granting of legislative seats, as strategies for preventing potential rivals from mounting a challenge to the regime (Arriola, DeVaro, and Meng 2021; Gandhi 2008). The idea that elite opponents can be co-opted in such ways rings true. Yet because cabinets are small and positions in the legislature are limited, such mechanisms can only be used to neutralize a relatively narrow circle of potential elite challengers. By contrast, political parties and state-sponsored mass organizations provide a more capacious tool for wide-ranging rival incorporation (Magaloni 2006; Brownlee 2007; Geddes, Wright, and Frantz 2018, 131–136). In particular, parties can attract and retain ambitious individuals through the hierarchical assignment of services and benefits (Svolik 2012, 162–195). Large nationwide social organizations can play a similar role (Fulbrook 2005, 235–249). However, the latter control fewer resources, which correspondingly limits their capacity to incorporate potential rivals. Therefore, political parties emerge as the key mechanism for co-opting substantial segments of the population in autocracies.

5.1.1 The Organizational Advantage of Leninist Parties

Although any type of party can attempt rival incorporation, Leninist parties have an important advantage that stems from their organizational structure. Such parties governed in the ten communist states that collapsed in 1989–91, continue to rule in the five communist regimes that persist to the current day, and were in power in Taiwan prior to democratization (Dickson 1997). Leninist parties are hierarchically organized and aim to achieve both vertical depth and horizontal breadth. Depth is ensured through party cells that operate at every level of the administrative system, all the way down to the grassroots. Breadth requires a wide sectoral penetration, which can be accomplished by establishing a party presence in all government offices; in all types of firms; in all educational institutions; and in all types of social organizations. One consequence of such an organizational design is that Leninist parties will grow over time, possibly exceeding 10 percent of the total population. This growth is a key metric of the successful incorporation of wide segments of society into the party. The alternative, which involves individuals leaving the party and creating opposition political movements, is a sign of regime decay and an indicator of a higher probability of collapse.

5.2 Expanding the Size of the Party

In August 1989, as widespread disaffection with the CCP was palpable, General Secretary Jiang Zemin paid a visit to the Organization Department to stress the importance of party building (Zhonggong Zhongyang Zuzhi Bu 2021b, 322). Consequently, although the population has increased by only 30 percent since 1989, the CCP has doubled in size during that same period. This reveals the zeal with which the Organization Department has approached the task of vertical and horizontal party expansion in the aftermath of the Tiananmen Square protests. Although its existence may sometimes not be apparent to casual observers, the CCP is omnipresent. Its universal reach allows for the identification of potential troublemakers and their incorporation into the ranks, where they can be controlled more effectively than if they were to remain outside the party.

5.2.1 General Trends in Party Building, 1989–2023

The Organization Department of the CCP is often considered to be one of the nerve centers of the party (Shambaugh 2008; McGregor 2010). This reflects the outsized importance of the department in party building, broadly construed – a paramount task that involves not only creating new party cells but also expanding the size of the CCP and staffing government bureaucracies with party cadres through the *nomenklatura* system. When evaluating the post-Tiananmen record of the Organization Department, we should note three trends that are indicative of strength: a growing membership roster; a higher number of party structures; and increased levels of education among CCP members. At the same time, these achievements in party building are counterbalanced by the movement of the party away from a mass-based to an elite-oriented organization; the rapid aging of its membership; and the significant drop in applications to join the CCP. Signs of dynamism and indicia of potential ossification are present simultaneously, thus creating uncertainty about the party's continued success in rival incorporation.

To begin, the party has registered remarkable increases in its membership. Between 1989 and the end of 2023, the CCP doubled in size from 49.5 million to 99.2 million members (see Figure 3). Most noteworthy about this development is that it took place against the background of the collapse of the communist regimes in Eastern Europe and Mongolia. The CCP studied this demise extensively at the time it occurred and today it continues to remind party cadres of the lessons that should be drawn from it, key among which is the imperative of maintaining organizational strength (Xiang 2018). In contrast to Eastern Europe, the party in China not only survived but thrived. Based on its size, the CCP today appears to be stronger than ever.

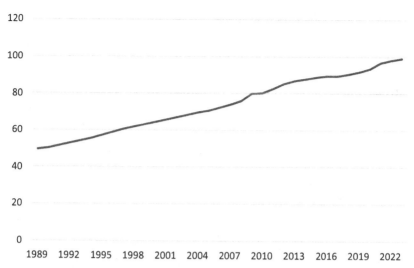

Figure 3 Chinese Communist Party membership, 1989–2023 (millions).
Sources: Zhonggong Zhongyang Zuzhi Bu 2011, 9–10; 2013–24.

Further evidence of vitality is provided by statistics on the development of party structures throughout the country. In China, there are three types of party organizations. According to the Party Constitution, when at least three party members are present, a party branch (*zhibu*) can be formed. Party branches can have a maximum of fifty members. In situations where more than 50 but fewer than 100 members exist, a general branch (*zong zhibu*) can be created. Party committees (*dangwei*) are established in units that have at least 100 members. Table 2 presents evidence of the success in setting up party organizations, whose number grew by two-thirds between 1989 and the end of 2023.

The educational level of CCP members is also increasing. As Table 3 reveals, communist party members were overwhelmingly illiterate in 1949. Yet, illiteracy in the CCP had been nearly wiped out by 2000. As the share of illiterate party members has declined, the number of those with an associate degree (*dazhuan*) or a higher degree increased. In the three decades following 1989, the proportion of CCP members with advanced degrees quintupled. By 2023, more than one-half of party members had advanced degrees. The trend is unmistakable: the CCP in the twenty-first century is a party of educated individuals rather than of illiterates. In contrast, only 15.47 percent of the population overall had an associate degree or higher, according to the 2020 Census (www.stats.gov.cn).

The improved quality of party members is linked to another phenomenon, with less clear implications for the future of the CCP. Simply put, this is no

Table 2 Party organizational development (selected years)

	1989	2000	2013	2023
Party branches	2,803,398	3,161,338	3,835,000	4,554,000
Party general branches	130,928	187,331	265,000	325,000
Party committees	135,545	169,053	203,000	298,000
Total	3,069,871	3,517,722	4,304,000	5,176,000

Sources: Zhonggong Zhongyang Zuzhi Bu 2002, 176; 2014 (rounding errors reproduced as found in source); 2024.

Table 3 Educational attainment of party members

	1949	1989	2000	2023
Illiterate	69%	7.3%	2.5%	
Associate's degree or higher	0.3%	9.7%	21.1%	56.2%

Sources: Zhonggong Zhongyang Zuzhi Bu 2002, 50–53; 2024.

Table 4 Share of workers and peasants in the party

	1949	1989	2000	2023
Workers	2.5%	13%	11.4%	6.7%
Peasants	59.6%	37.5%	32.4%	26.3%

Sources: Zhonggong Zhongyang Zuzhi Bu 2002, 98–105; 2024.

longer a party of workers and peasants. Table 4 illustrates the change over time. In 1949, the two groups made up over 60 percent of the party membership. By 1989, they accounted for one-half. And in 2023, they constituted a mere one-third. A party that is composed of professionals, managers, businesspeople, and government bureaucrats is in danger of becoming elite-oriented rather than mass-oriented. Time will tell how serious those fissures are and how they might impact the capacity of the party to present itself as defending the interests of the masses.

Another trend that calls into question the vitality of the party is the aging of its members. We can illustrate the problem by contrasting the share of party members aged thirty-five or younger and those aged sixty-one or older. Table 5 allows us to trace how these proportions have evolved since 1989. It is beyond any doubt that the party has become older in a way that is even more extreme than the general aging of Chinese society (as revealed by the last population census

Table 5 Young and elderly individuals in the CCP (1989 and 2021) vs. in the general population over 18 years of age

	1989 CCP members	2021 CCP members	General population over 18
35 or younger	23.9%	25%	27.9%
61 or older	11.5%	28.1%	24%

Sources: Zhonggong Zhongyang Zuzhi Bu 2002, 24–25; 2022; www.stats.gov.cn.

conducted in 2020). When we interpret the statistics, we should also consider that, as of 2024, the standard retirement age in China remains age fifty-five for women and age sixty for men (though it will be gradually raised to fifty-eight for women and sixty-three for men by the end of 2039). Although individuals of any age are potential challengers to the regime, those who are younger tend to be more likely to cause trouble. Thus, a party whose base is increasingly skewed toward retirees is less capable of rival incorporation.

A final source of concern is the declining number of applicants to join the CCP. We should note that becoming a party member is not automatic. Rather, it involves a formal application and a complex vetting process, which culminates into the status of a candidate member (*yubei dangyuan*). According to Article 7 of the Party Constitution, candidate members are formally allowed to join the party (*rudang*) as full members only after a one-year probationary period. As Figure 4 illustrates, the decline became noticeable in 2016, when the number of applicants dropped by 8.5 percent as compared to 2015. In 2017–19, there was a further erosion of interest in party membership. The Organization Department remains silent about the cause of this issue. One interpretation is that the population of young adults (who form the largest share of the pool of potential party members) is shrinking. While it is undeniable that there has been a steady decline in the number of young individuals, this factor cannot account for the timing of such a sharp drop. A more likely explanation is a rational reaction to the reduced quota for new members that was implemented in 2015. It is clear that even if the party wants to slow down its growth, this should not occur at the cost of declining interest in joining, as revealed by the drop in applications. In this light, the uptick in applications in 2021–23 is perhaps a source of hope for the CCP, though it remains to be seen whether it is a temporary effect of the 2021 centenary celebrations, when the quota for new party members was relaxed (it was restricted again in 2022–23). We will revisit the implications of some of these trends for the future of the party in the conclusion to this section of the Element.

Figure 4 Applications for party membership, 2009–2023 (millions).
Sources: Zhonggong Zhongyang Zuzhi Bu 2014–24; Cui and Chen 2016, 37.

5.2.2 The Party in Educational Institutions

Perhaps unsurprisingly, the CCP has established a formidable presence in educational institutions. Given China's history of destabilizing student unrest in 1919 and 1989, maintaining firm control over universities is seen as especially important (Yan 2014; Perry 2020). Available statistics indicate that by 2000, only three of the 1,041 institutions of higher learning (0.29 percent) had not yet formed party committees, general branches, or branches (Zhonggong Zhongyang Zuzhi Bu 2002, 213). The monitoring of students remains a paramount concern to the current day, thus necessitating an ongoing party presence on university campuses. This may explain why Qinghua and other leading universities officially announced in 2024 the merger of their party and university administrations.[7] One issue that has not been explained is the operation of party committees at foreign universities in China. As they often employ Chinese nationals (many of whom are CCP members), they too must have party organizations, but their existence is not publicized to international students and to foreign teaching staff. A similar secretiveness applies to party cells on US and other overseas campuses. Although the existence of party committees at Harvard and Oxford is almost certain, it is not publicly acknowledged. The CCP prefers to operate *sub rosa* in foreign educational institutions, typically under the cover of the Chinese Students and Scholars Association (Yan and Alsudairi 2021, 814). Beyond surveillance at

---

[7] www.rfa.org/mandarin/yataibaodao/kejiaowen/gt2-01172024011658.html.

home and abroad, the party is also in charge of indoctrinating students with Marxism–Leninism to ward off the influence of foreign ideas spread through the Internet (Lu 2020).

5.2.3 The Party in NGOs

The conventional understanding is that NGOs should be independent of the party-state and should facilitate democratization (Bernhard 1993; Ekiert 1996). Western political science has paid substantial attention to civil-society groups under authoritarianism in light of their demonstrated capacity to catalyze opposition to the regime and to drive political change (Kubik 1994; Jancar-Webster 1998; Nepstad 2011). Although NGOs in China had a golden age when interference in their work was sporadic and therefore minimal in some cases, that period came to an end in the 1990s (Saich 2000). NGOs are now allowed to operate only if they supply social services (such as education, healthcare, elder care, or poverty alleviation) in cases where state provision is insufficient to meet demand, if they remain local rather than seeking to establish a nationwide network, and if they refrain from voicing calls for democracy (Spires 2011; Hsu 2017). Since the 2000s and especially in the 2010s, requirements for registration with the state authorities have been stringently enforced. In general, successful NGOs must display a cooperative attitude toward the state (Teets 2014).

The autonomy of civil organizations has been constrained not only by tighter state regulatory control but also by the requirement that they establish party organizations, as mandated by the CCP Organization Department (Hu, Zeng, and Wu 2022; Wang and Wang 2023). Although these rules have been in place since 1998, they were not rigorously enforced until after the Eighteenth Party Congress in 2012 (Zhou 2018; Xin and Huang 2022). Since then, party branches, general branches, and party committees have been established at civil-society organizations (*shehui zuzhi*), a term that includes civic associations, NGOs, and private foundations. Figure 5 illustrates the growth of party structures at civil-society organizations during the 2012–23 period. One feature of party building that is revealed in Figure 5 but has not been discussed by the CCP Organization Department, is that the number of party structures declined after 2017. It is especially noteworthy that this reduction occurred as the number of NGOs increased from 761,539 in 2017 to 891,267 in 2022 (*Zhongguo tongji nianjian* 2023, 728). What might be driving this? The closure of foreign NGOs is unlikely to account for the general decline in party structures, as such NGOs make up well under 1 percent of all registered social organizations in China (China NGO Project 2022; *Zhongguo tongji nianjian* 2023, 728). A more plausible explanation is that the Organization Department

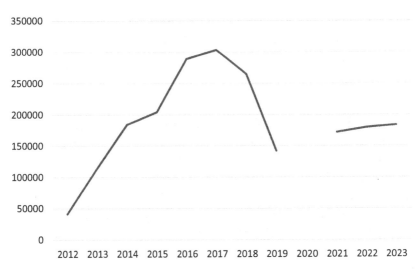

Figure 5 Party structures in civil-society organizations, 2012–2023.
Source: Zhonggong Zhongyang Zuzhi Bu 2013–24.

was reacting to the fivefold increase in party structures in NGOs between 2012 and 2015 with alarm and therefore decided to merge some inefficient independent party branches (*duli zhibu*) into joint party branches (*lianhe zhibu*) that share a supervisory unit (e.g., the Federation of Industry and Commerce), belong to the same type of industry (e.g., a league of Internet firms), or are territorially concentrated (e.g., in streets, industrial parks, or buildings).[8] This policy was promulgated at the end of 2015, but implementation took some time, thus not leading to a perceptible drop in party structures in NGOs until after 2017.

What does this mean for the panoptical capacity of the party? In 2017, the Organization Department reported that 61.7 percent of civil-society organizations had established a party organization (Zhonggong Zhongyang Zuzhi Bu 2018). Alternative calculations based on officially released numbers reveal that only 39.8 percent of NGOs had a party branch in 2017 (Xin and Huang 2022, 429). Using Xin and Huang's methodology (2022), we can extend their analysis beyond 2017 to discover that the share of NGOs with party committees declined to as low as 16 percent in 2019 before rebounding to 20 percent in 2022 (Zhonggong Zhongyang Zuzhi Bu 2018–23; *Zhongguo tongji nianjian* 2023, 728). The communist leadership understands the potential of social organizations to challenge the system. For this reason, the CCP seeks to keep NGOs under strict control and surveillance. The implications of the drop in the number of NGOs with party cells revealed in Figure 5 deserve future attention.

---

[8] http://dangjian.people.com.cn/n/2015/0929/c117092-27645046.html.

5.2.4 The Party in Private Firms

Although various regulations mandating the creation of party committees in joint ventures and private enterprises of a certain size were promulgated by the CCP Organization Department in the 1980s and 1990s, enforcement was inconsistent to the end of the 1990s (Holbig 2004; Chen 2008). This changed in 2000–01 with the doctrinal adjustment articulated in Jiang Zemin's theory of the Three Represents, which allowed the entry of capitalists into the CCP (Shambaugh 2008). Through a policy of concurrent appointment (*jiaocha renzhi*), private entrepreneurs may also serve as the party secretaries at their enterprises. By 2010, 70 percent of the capitalists who were also CCP members were assuming the functions of party secretaries at their respective firms (Yan and Huang 2017, 52). Beginning in 2012, the Organization Department started to devote considerable attention to extend the party's presence at both domestic and foreign private firms, singling out Internet companies for special attention (Xue 2018). The party's determination to penetrate private business is palpable (Koss 2021).

One issue that has not yet received sufficient attention is the precise extent to which the CCP has infiltrated private business. In part, this is due to changes in the way that data are reported. From 1998 to 2010, internal party statistical compendia tracked the number of party members at nonstate enterprises, which included private enterprises; Hong Kong, Macau, and Taiwan-invested enterprises; and foreign-invested enterprises. According to this standard, 3,526,676 CCP members worked in the above three types of nonstate enterprises as of 2010 (Zhonggong Zhongyang Zuzhi Bu 2011, 198). This is equivalent to 4.4 percent of CCP members at the time.

After 2010, the unit of accounting was changed from the individual to the firm, using the preexisting three-way breakdown of nonstate firms. Figure 6 illustrates the record of party building at private firms during the past decade. By 2015, as many as 1,602,000 firms (constituting 51.8 percent of the total that were required to do so according to CCP regulations) had established party organizations (*dang zuzhi*) (Zhonggong Zhongyang Zuzhi Bu 2016). After peaking in 2017 (when 1,877,000 firms or 73.1 percent of the total number of enterprises with the requisite number of party members had a CCP presence),[9] the number of firms with party organizations declined to 1,585,000 in 2018, representing a 15.5 percent drop from 2017 (Zhonggong Zhongyang Zuzhi Bu 2018–19). This decline, which continued in 2019, has not been noted in either the English-language or the Chinese scholarly literature. As the number of

---

[9] We should note that the total number of private firms in that year was 14.4 million (*Zhongguo tongji nianjian* 2018).

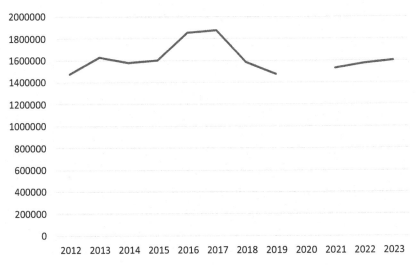

Figure 6 Party organizations in private firms, 2012–2023.
Source: Zhonggong Zhongyang Zuzhi Bu 2013–24.

private firms was continuing to increase, the most likely cause was not the bankruptcies but rather the policies, promulgated in 2016, that required the merger of party branches according to supervisory unit, industry, or region. The impact of such policies began to be visible shortly thereafter.[10] The parallel with NGOs is not coincidental: NGOs and private firms are managed by the same "two-new" (*liangxin*) work committee of the Organization Department. This under-resourced work committee faces immense pressures to find entities willing to serve as supervisory units for party branches in NGOs and private firms (Wang Jingqing 2021, 159–176). Loosely federated party branches have emerged as one response to the practical problem of insufficient resources within the Organization Department to manage independent party branches. Careful analysis of further data will be necessary to evaluate the implications of these developments for the capacity of the CCP to maintain a panoptical vision and tight control over private firms.

5.3 Problems of Rival Incorporation

The achievements in party building detailed in Section 5.2 notwithstanding, the CCP is facing difficulties penetrating certain groups, with corresponding implications for successful rival incorporation. We will focus specifically on ethnic minorities; intellectuals who are critical of the system; and Hong Kong and Macau residents.

---

[10] http://dangjian.people.com.cn/n1/2016/0818/c117092-28646759.html.

5.3.1 Penetration of Ethnic Minorities

The situation for ethnic minorities is complex (Leibold 2020; Roberts 2020). On the one hand, since 1989 the CCP has been recruiting minorities at a rapid pace. The available statistics, as presented in Figure 7, indicate that the overall share of minorities is increasing, reaching 7.7 percent in 2023, which is an all-time high and is comparable to the 8.9 percent share of minorities in the overall population.[11]

At the same time, a more nuanced picture emerges when we examine the situation with regard to representation of various different minorities. Table 6

Table 6 Percentage of ethnic groups in the general population and among party members (2006)

Ethnic group	Population %	CCP %
Han	91.6%	93.6%
Uyghur	0.7%	0.5%
Tibetan	0.5%	0.4%
Mongol	0.4%	0.5%
Korean	0.1%	0.2%

Sources: Zhonggong Zhongyang Zuzhi Bu 2011, 194; Chinese census data.

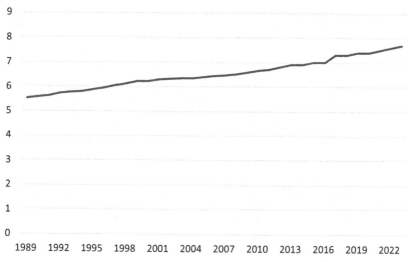

Figure 7 Percentage shares of ethnic minorities in the Chinese Communist Party, 1989–2023.

Sources: Zhonggong Zhongyang Zuzhi Bu 2011, 9–10; 2013–24.

---

[11] www.cia.gov/the-world-factbook/countries/china/.

demonstrates that CCP members from quiescent ethnic groups like the Koreans are overrepresented in the party (as is the Han Chinese majority), whereas restive minorities like the Uyghurs and the Tibetans are underrepresented. The only data point we have on this very sensitive issue is from 2006. This makes it difficult to assess whether the situation has changed, though the high level of discontent among these minority groups does not augur well for the capacity of the CCP to recruit from among them. Historically, minorities were underrepresented both in party school training courses and among CCP members in Xinjiang (Xinjiang 1990, 189–190; Xinjiang 2022, 3). The failure of co-optation in turn has implications for resorting to repression to manage minority threats.

5.3.2 Intellectuals Critical of the System

The Eastern European communist regimes were known for their robust dissident movements. This is probably best exemplified by Czech playwright Václav Havel, whose Charter 77 became a human-rights manifesto that helped accelerate the collapse of the system. Though keenly studied by outside observers, Chinese dissidents, like Wei Jingsheng, Fang Lizhi, Wang Dan, Liu Xiaobo, Chen Guangcheng, and Teng Biao, never achieved a domestic profile commensurate with that of Havel in Czechoslovakia. When Chinese dissidents emerged, they were silenced by either imprisonment or exile, thus limiting their capacity to speak meaningfully to domestic audiences and to foment anti-regime mobilization. But perhaps even more important is that, with only a few exceptions, the CCP has been successful at incorporating potential critics (Tismaneanu 2013). The last decade has presented a test of the capacity of the regime to handle human-rights defenders who were operating outside the party. This threat was eventually dealt with through repression, as illustrated by the fourteen- and twelve-year sentences given to prominent activists Xu Zhiyong and Ding Jiaxi respectively, in April 2023, for subversion of state power.

As we think about the future of China, we need to be mindful that its prior success in handling these challengers through incorporation and repression is no guarantee that the strategy will continue to be effective. This lesson is not lost on the CCP, which has carefully studied both foreign examples of dissidence and its domestic manifestations. We can be certain that the party will remain vigilant about the threats posed by dissidents, human-rights defenders, and intellectuals critical of the system.

5.3.3 Penetration in Hong Kong and Macau

Although Hong Kong and Macau became SARs of the PRC in 1997 and 1999, respectively, the CCP continues to operate underground in both places. No statistics have been released on the number of party members in either of the two jurisdictions, but more is known about the CCP in Hong Kong, which has been a more problematic region. Compared to Macau, it is bigger; more independence-minded; and less trusting of the center. The party in Hong Kong historically operated under the guise of the New China (Xinhua) News Agency and since 2000 under the Liaison Office of the Central People's Government (Loh 2018). The CCP supports the Democratic Alliance for the Betterment of Hong Kong, which is the largest political party in Hong Kong. The party also maintains very close links with the Federation of Trade Unions (Pepper 2021) and has control over both traditional and online media (Burns 2022). However, as these ties are not officially acknowledged, much remains unknown about the party's presence: How widely is the *nomenklatura* system used for key appointments (Burns 1990; 2022)? Does the party have a presence in government institutions? How deeply have firms, educational institutions, and social organizations been penetrated? And, above all, how many CCP members are there in Hong Kong? For the time being, the CCP remains an underground organization in both Hong Kong and Macau, thus making it difficult to assess with precision its organizational strength (Loh 2018; Pepper 2021).

As we turn to the future, we can make several observations. To start, Macau does not present a problem for the CCP. It remained quiescent even when Hong Kong was engulfed by a democracy movement (Geddes 2020). With regard to Hong Kong, the further expansion of pro-Beijing parties and social organizations is a certainty. Tycoons will presumably remain co-opted. At the same time, the CCP's capacity for rival incorporation is limited, as evidenced by the brutal clampdown on the waves of pro-democracy protests throughout the 2010s and the imposition of the National Security Law in 2020. Instead of co-optation, the CCP has adopted harsh repression to be used against its most outspoken political opponents. Installing John Lee, a former police officer, as chief executive of the SAR in 2022 speaks to the grim future that awaits Hong Kong.

5.4 Auxiliary Mechanisms for Rival Incorporation

Within the PRC, there exist three additional mechanisms for rival incorporation: the All-China Women's Federation; the All-China Federation of Trade Unions; and the United Front. The All-China Women's Federation has a deep grassroots presence, with as many as 685,000 local organizations. It provides employment opportunities for 7.8 million executive members,[12] thus helping with the incorporation of potentially disgruntled female citizens.

---

[12] www.womenofchina.cn/womenofchina/html1/about/1503/2333-1.htm.

The main function of the All-China Federation of Trade Unions is to prevent the emergence of alternative trade unions. After all, regime insiders are fully aware of the role that the independent trade union Solidarity played in Poland's democratization process. Prior to its being banned in 1981, Solidarity boasted ten million members in a country of thirty-six million. To maintain its clout, the All-China Federation of Trade Unions seeks to establish a deep grassroots presence and a large membership base: in 2017, there were 2,829,000 grassroots trade union organizations with 302 million members.[13] By 2020, there were 2,196,000 grassroots organizations with an undisclosed number of members (85 million members were recruited in the three years since 2017).[14] The long-term implications of the decline in the number of trade unions has not been analyzed in the literature. They deserve further study.

The United Front Work Department of the CCP has a long history that goes back to the pre-1949 collaboration with the Guomindang (KMT) (Van Slyke 1967). The United Front persisted after the 1949 revolution and survives to the current day. It has a wide purview that includes managing the eight minor parties: the Jiusan Society; the China Democratic League; the China Zhigong Party; the Revolutionary KMT; the China National Democratic Construction Association; the China Association for Promoting Democracy; the Chinese Peasants and Workers Democratic Party; and the Taiwan Democratic Self-Government League. Officially known as "democratic," these eight parties had a combined membership of 1.3 million in 2020, representing a tripling since 1996 (Groot 2004, 185). These parties play a limited role in rival incorporation by controlling 372 of the 2,980 seats in the National People's Congress (2018 data); some seats in the Chinese People's Political Consultative Conference; and seats in the subnational legislatures. Scholars have found that the allocation of legislative positions is an effective strategy of incorporation, especially of entrepreneurs (Hou 2019; Zhang 2021).

The United Front Work Department also controls the All-China Federation of Industry and Commerce and the chambers of commerce, which work jointly under the "one organization, two nameplates" principle (Groot 2004, 191). In 2018, there existed 3,416 industry and commerce federations and 48,916 chambers of commerce, with 2.6 million enterprise members.[15] The federations and chambers of commerce are used to create bridges to ambitious entrepreneurs and to ensure that they ultimately remain loyal to the CCP (Zhang 2021). They are also one of the entities in charge of party building in private firms (Wang Jingqing 2021, 173). In short, both the United Front

---

[13] http://acftu.people.com.cn/n1/2017/0410/c197470-29200210.html.

[14] www.acftu.org/wjzl/ldjh/qtsjcld/202108/t20210803_784359.html.

[15] www.chinachamber.org.cn/About_Us/.

Work Department and the CCP-controlled All-China Women's Federation and All-China Federation of Trade Unions are used as auxiliary institutions for rival incorporation.

5.5 Conclusion: Has the CCP Reached the Limit of Its Potential Growth?

This section has reviewed the strategies deployed by the CCP to incorporate potential rivals into the party. Signs of success abound: the party has grown and expanded into universities, private firms, and NGOs. No alternative political organization has arisen since the quashing of the Democracy Party of China in 1998. And unlike in Poland, where Solidarity challenged communist rule, no independent trade union movement has been allowed to emerge in China. Yet, there are reasons for concern. The CCP is becoming more elitist, older, and less popular, judging from the number of annual applications for membership. Its capacity to incorporate minorities, intellectuals who are critical of the system, and residents of Hong Kong and Macau is limited. Finally, Chinese opinion polling shows that levels of trust both in government and in party officials are declining (*Lingdao Canyue* 2014; Li, Chen, and Zhang 2015, 123). All this spells potential trouble in the future as the party aims to co-opt additional challengers. To stay in power, the CCP will need to continue to grow and to absorb those who might threaten its rule.

As we consider the future, one remaining question is whether the party has reached the natural limit of its expansion. Comparative data help shed some light on this issue. A large party is the most useful tool for policy implementation and for safeguarding ideological purity in a communist regime. Party building therefore is a central priority for the leadership. Yet the voluminous literature on comparative communism has not identified a basic empirical fact, namely, that regimes born from revolution develop smaller communist parties than regimes created through imposition. This surprising finding contradicts influential arguments that emphasize the organizational strength of revolutionary parties (Levitsky and Way 2022). The precise mechanism that can explain this result awaits future theorization, although plausible hypotheses must begin with the fact that communist political movements were illegal prior to the revolution, thus forcing them to survive as small underground organizations. By contrast, in nonrevolutionary regimes communist parties were legal, meaning that they had to compete against other parties in elections, which allowed them to engage in party building prior to the imposition of communist rule. The effects of regime type persist over time: party size in

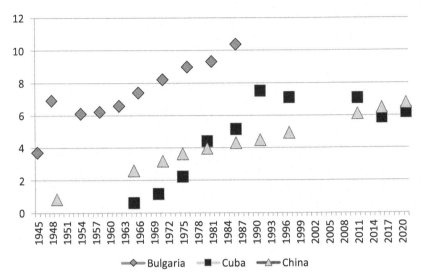

Figure 8 Party size in China, Cuba, and Bulgaria (as a percentage of the population).

Sources: Tsvetanski 1988, 29; Zhonggong Zhongyang Zuzhi Bu 2011 and 2013–22; *Informe Central* of the First through the Eighth Congress of the Cuban Communist Party (available at www.pcc.cu/es).

revolutionary regimes remains consistently smaller than in nonrevolutionary regimes (Dimitrov 2024).

A specific empirical illustration of these claims is useful. As Figure 8 shows, revolutionary regimes like China and Cuba had substantially smaller parties during their initial decade of rule than did a nonrevolutionary regime like Bulgaria. However, due to vigorous party building, in 2021 China and Cuba had communist parties that accounted for, respectively, 6.76 percent and 6.18 percent of the population. This is similar to the Communist Party of the Soviet Union at the height of its development in 1988, when its membership accounted for 6.83 percent of the Soviet population. Yet, we should not allow those statistics to obscure the consequential fact of the decline in party size in Cuba, from 7.05 percent of the population in 2011 to 5.84 percent in 2016. Although it rebounded slightly to 6.18 percent in 2021, the Cuban Communist Party has surpassed its maximum size. In light of this finding and the 2014 decision to limit the annual quota of new CCP members, we might wonder whether we have witnessed a peak in the size of the CCP, which reached 7 percent in 2023. Given the negative implications for successful rival incorporation, this would represent a troubling prospect for the Organization Department and the top leadership. While there are no clear guidelines on what the optimal party size might be, a bigger party that manages to maintain high-quality members is, in general, more desirable than a smaller party, as the larger size allows for more expansive control. The worst outcome is when individuals renounce their party membership en masse, as occurred in Poland in the 1980s and elsewhere in the Eastern Bloc in the 1990s. This is not a fate the CCP would want to experience.

6 Conclusion

This Element has analyzed four adaptations deployed by the CCP in response to the domestic and international shocks sustained by China's single-party political system in 1989. This concluding section will briefly review the four adaptations and argue that each of them is undergoing strains that create doubts about its future viability. The crisis in adaptability, which has become palpable during the Xi administration, has been accompanied by an increase in physical and digital repression. However, harsh repression cannot be an effective long-term governance strategy in a sophisticated authoritarian regime like China. Considering that political liberalization is not on the limited menu of available adaptations, China's future is uncertain. The urgent question that emerges from this concluding section is how much longer can a repressive regime in which adaptation has ossified survive?

6.1 Adaptations and Their Limits in Post-1989 China

Without a doubt, 1989 ushered in a period of deep introspection for the CCP, which took the time to evaluate the reasons for the domestic upheaval and for the collapse of communist regimes around the world. The lessons learned guided the adaptations undertaken after 1989, with the explicit aim of shoring up the single-party model.

One conclusion that emerges is that 1989 was driven by socioeconomic uncertainty. This was well on display in Tiananmen Square, where the workers were protesting about inflation and job insecurity separately from the students who were demanding a more consultative type of leadership. The dilemma was how to restructure the inefficient SOEs without the attendant massive social costs. The solution has been to pursue economic reforms and to allow the private sector to grow, but to postpone the politically explosive SOE reforms for nearly a decade. In the late 1990s, Chinese SOEs underwent a process of controlled partial privatization, which allowed the CCP to mitigate the negative side effects, such as the loss of employment or welfare benefits. Concurrently, pensions, healthcare, and unemployment insurance were extended to increasingly wider segments of the population. Thus, the genesis of the first two adaptations (controlled SOE restructuring and welfare reforms) can be traced directly to 1989.

This is also true with regard to the third adaptation, which stemmed from ideological insecurities due to exposure to foreign ideas about democracy and human rights. The desire to limit the impact of external ideological influences led to a defensive approach of blocking those vectors that would allow foreign ideas to penetrate the country and to a counteroffensive strategy of building a domestic cultural industry and of displacing interest in Western cultural products by promoting indigenous cultural consumption. Though it existed prior to 1989, the concept of cultural security was reinvigorated by the Tiananmen events and by the collapse of communism in Eastern Europe.

The final adaptation was also driven by the Tiananmen events. It became apparent to the CCP in 1989 that political pluralism must be avoided at all costs because once a multiparty system is permitted, collapse of the communist regime will inevitably follow. The response of the CCP has been to enhance its efforts to maintain both its depth and its breadth of penetration. The party doubled in size after 1989 and it managed to establish a presence in educational institutions, NGOs, and private firms, thus neutralizing groups like students, civil-society activists, and entrepreneurs who potentially could pose a challenge.

These four adaptations have allowed the CCP to extend its lifespan. Yet, each is now showing signs of decreasing effectiveness. Economic reform has stagnated. That the superrich are faced with property and personal insecurities is particularly worrying. Although it is currently unlikely that the superrich will mount an organized challenge against the CCP in an effort to defend their wealth (Markus 2015), the offensive against private corporations will inevitably depress growth. This may be why attitudes toward oligarchs were relaxed somewhat in 2023. The second adaptation of welfare extension is also malfunctioning. The problem here is that because of the ineffectiveness of the petitioning system, citizens have been using protests to articulate their welfare grievances, which were often directed against rapacious local governments that were acting in concert with unscrupulous businesses that were unwilling to provide the welfare to which the citizenry was entitled. Even worse, cash-strapped local governments authorized lucrative redevelopment projects that involved land grabs and the illegal destruction of housing (both land and housing are considered fundamental welfare rights in China). Prior to the Xi administration, an equilibrium was maintained whereby the government showed a sufficient level of responsiveness to the demands of protesters. After Xi assumed power, a repressive turn led to prioritizing the dispersing of protesters rather than satisfying their demands (Cai and Chen 2022). Such a lack of responsiveness to citizen grievances has alarming implications for the future. Frustrations cannot be suppressed indefinitely.

Cultural security is also under strain. In September 2021, the Propaganda Department, through the National Radio and TV Administration, banned broadcasters from airing content featuring "sissy men and other abnormal esthetics" (Voice of America 2021). This was the final salvo of a heated debate in the Chinese media in 2019–21 about the cult following of androgynous male pop idols like Zhu Zhengting and Liu Yu and the national security implications of the esthetic phenomenon variously labeled "sissies" (*niangpao*) and somewhat affectionately "little fresh meat" (*xiao xianrou*). In October 2019, the official blog of the National Cultural Security and Ideological Construction Research Center of the Chinese Academy of Social Sciences argued that the current popularity of androgynous stars in China, Korea, and Japan can be traced back to a 1980s CIA plot to promote effeminate entertainers in East Asia, in contrast to the virile masculinity projected by the US creative arts industry. The blogpost left no doubt that the alarming spread of *niangpao* presents a threat to Chinese cultural security. Leaving aside the offensive language used by propagandists to describe the pop stars, the practical implications of banning popular domestic content are alarming. Considering that the very rationale for promoting indigenous cultural production was that it would displace interest in Western culture and would thus ensure ideological security, banning Chinese pop idols appears to be a self-defeating strategy.

Finally, the CCP is changing in ways that may not be conducive to its continued role as a highly effective mechanism for rival incorporation. The party is becoming more elitist, older, and less popular. None of these trends bodes well for the future.

In light of the ossification of the existing adaptations, what might be the way forward? Taking into account that China has no interest in political pluralism or in initiating a process of democratization from strength (Slater and Wong 2022), we might wonder whether there are other major adaptations that we have not discussed. In a volume published a decade ago (Dimitrov 2013), I highlight four adaptive responses that explain the resilience of the five surviving communist regimes (China, Vietnam, Laos, North Korea, and Cuba). In addition to deploying repression, these countries all undertook at least some of the following adaptations: of the economy; of ideology; of the mechanisms for inclusion; and of the systems for accountability. These were more general versions of the post-1989 China-specific adaptations discussed in this Element: economic reform; cultural (ideological) security; inclusion (rival incorporation), primarily through the CCP; and, as one element of accountability, responsiveness to welfare grievances as articulated through petitions and protests. The general point is that the adaptations undertaken after 1989 were very carefully considered and the four discussed in this Element helped to prolong the lifespan of the CCP. Now that they are all malfunctioning, the party has turned to repression.

6.2 The Limits of Repression as a Mechanism for Ensuring the Longevity of Single-Party Rule

There is no doubt that China is capable of wielding technologically assisted repression (Qian et al. 2022). When we think about digital authoritarianism, we need to distinguish smart-city projects (using cameras, 5G technology, and the Internet-of-Things to deliver more efficient municipal services) from safe-city projects, which rely on technologically enabled surveillance to track individuals who may engage in politically subversive behavior. Safe cities employ hardware, software, and human intelligence to deploy sophisticated urban grid policing (Huang and Tsai 2021; Chen and Greitens 2022; Xu and He 2022). Piloted in a handful of coastal cities in the early 2000s, the so-called "grid-management system" (*wanggehua guanli*) was implemented throughout the Tibet Autonomous Region under Chen Quanguo's watch as party secretary in 2011–16 and it was later expanded to Xinjiang when Chen became party secretary there in 2016 (Leibold 2020). Today, urban grid policing is practiced throughout Chinese cities. Surveillance has been extended to rural areas as well through the Sharp Eyes (*xueliang*) Project. AI and smart policing continue to evolve, with camera density increasing at a constant pace. Other initiatives, such as the social credit system (Tsai, Wang, and Lin 2021) and blacklists are also expanding, even though there are questions about how well the different bureaucratic and regional blacklists are integrated and whether they can meaningfully be used to exert social control by naming and shaming those who engage in transgressive behavior (Arsène 2019; Jee 2022). Future advances in AI may enable more rapid and more precise response to protests that would make negotiation and compromise even less likely.

One question that we should examine is whether COVID-19 has introduced a major rupture in surveillance and information gathering. As of 2024, we can say that the pandemic did not function as a critical juncture in information collection. The ultra-intrusive surveillance for reasons of public health was repealed in 2023. However, the pre-pandemic systems persist and are continuously being upgraded. Perhaps the best illustration of the mélange of analog and digital practices is that community policing remains an important part of information gathering, reinforced through pre-pandemic upgrades of grid governance like the "constructing a peaceful China" initiative, as described in the Introduction to this Element. Grid policing relies on a high density of surveillance cameras and big data algorithms, but importantly, it also uses human intelligence collectors that enable a rapid reaction (Zhongyang Zhengfawei Bangongting 2021a). Visible and secret informants have not been made redundant by COVID-19 (Zhongyang Zhengfawei Bangongting 2021b).

Fundamentally, however, the question that is raised is whether repression can function as an effective long-term strategy to ensure regime resilience in China. There is no reason for the party leadership to think so. Although all autocracies are repressive, those that survive for a long period of time adopt selective repression (Dimitrov 2023). Neither sending millions of ethnic minorities to labor camps (as occurred in Xinjiang in the 2010s) nor implementing ubiquitous surveillance (with the potential to impose swift punishment) will be tolerated over the long term. Even if COVID-19 provided an excuse for extending surveillance further, eventually the pendulum swung back and pent-up frustrations were publicly expressed in the November–December 2022 protests, leading to the repeal of the zero-COVID policy that had resulted in severe mass lockdowns and widespread physical misery and psychological suffering for vast swaths of the Chinese population. Totalistic surveillance and mass repression, even under the guise of protecting public health, are ineffective long-term survival formulas.

6.3 Looking at the Future of the CCP

We end this Element on a mixed note. On the one hand, there is no denying the formidable achievements of the CCP, which has managed to stay in power for an extraordinarily long time. In 2023, the CCP matched the record of the Communist Party of the Soviet Union, which ruled for 74 years (1917–91). Most remarkable about the Chinese case is that the CCP has not only survived but it has thrived. While repression and ideological legitimacy may be sufficient for survival, as indicated by the North Korean experience, the Chinese formula of resilience has relied on the suite of adaptations reviewed in this volume. Implementing these adaptations has required considerable efforts on the part of Chinese leaders. Yet those adaptations have delivered extraordinary rewards in the form of communist regime resilience.

As the adaptations are ossifying and as the regime is unwilling to entertain ideas about political liberalization, the question of the future of China arises with great urgency. A decade into the Xi Jinping era, it is clear that repression has become harsher and more frequent. Although repression is used in all nondemocratic regimes, increases in the rate of deployment is a sign of weakness rather than strength. Autocracies with sophisticated governance mechanisms wield repression in a highly calculated, selective, and infrequent manner. This is not what we have witnessed in China since 2012. The implications of this repressive turn are worrying. While repression is essential for regime survival, resilience requires ongoing adaptation; this is one lesson we learned from the collapse of the single-party communist systems in 1989–91 and from the experience of those regimes that outlasted the Cold War.

Are there prospects for renewed CCP adaptation? The third term that Xi Jinping secured at the Twentieth Party Congress in 2022 will consolidate the repressive turn and will presumably lead to further ossification of the four adaptations highlighted in this Element. This will mean that China has opted for mere regime survival rather than for dynamic resilience. But political scientists need to be humble when prognosticating. The element of surprise (Kuran 1991) is what makes real-world events exciting and what helps us refine our theories. China has surprised us before. It may well do so again. Although empowering civil society and gradual political liberalization seem highly unlikely, reinvigorating adaptive governance and relaxing repression may lie in China's future.

Abbreviations

AI	artificial intelligence
CCP	Chinese Communist Party
FDI	foreign direct investment
GDP	gross domestic product
KMT	Guomindang
MPS	Ministry of Public Security
MSS	Ministry of State Security
NGO	nongovernmental organization
NSC	National Security Council
PRC	People's Republic of China
SAR	Special Administrative Region
SARS	Severe Acute Respiratory Syndrome
SASAC	State Asset Supervision Administration of China
SOE	state-owned enterprise
TVE	township and village enterprise
WTO	World Trade Organization

References

Alsudairi, Mohammed. 2019. "Fighting the Many Smoke-less Wars: A Comparative Study of the Origins, Conceptualizations and Practices of Cultural Security in China and Saudi Arabia." PhD Dissertation, University of Hong Kong.

Ang, Yuen Yuen. 2016. *How China Escaped the Poverty Trap*. Ithaca, NY: Cornell University Press.

2020. *China's Gilded Age: The Paradox of Economic Boom and Vast Corruption*. New York: Cambridge University Press.

Arendt, Hannah. 1951. *The Origins of Totalitarianism*. New York: Harcourt, Brace and Company.

Arriola, Leonardo R., Jed DeVaro, and Anne Meng. 2021. "Democratic Subversion: Elite Cooptation and Opposition Fragmentation." *American Political Science Review* 115 (4): 1358–1372.

Arsène, Séverine. 2019. "China's Social Credit System: A Chimera with Real Claws." Paris: Institut français des relations internationales.

Barmé, Geremie R. 2009. "China's Flat Earth: History and 8 August 2008." *The China Quarterly* 197: 64–86.

Barros, Robert. 2016. "On the Outside Looking In: Secrecy and the Study of Authoritarian Regimes." *Social Science Quarterly* 97 (4): 953–973.

Beijing Shi Difangzhi Bianzuan Weiyuanhui. 2020. *Beijing zhi: Gong'an zhi, 1986–2010*. Beijing: Beijing Chubanshe.

Beijing Shi Gong'an Ju. 2001. *Beijing gong'an nianjian 2001*. Beijing: Zhongguo Renmin Gong'an Daxue Chubanshe.

2014. *Beijing gong'an nianjian 2014*. Beijing: Beijing Anjixing Yinshuachang.

Bernhard, Michael. 1993. "Civil Society and Democratic Transition in East Central Europe." *Political Science Quarterly* 108 (2): 307–326.

Betts, Paul. 2010. *Within Walls: Private Life in the German Democratic Republic*. New York: Oxford University Press.

Blanchette, Jude. 2020. "From 'China Inc.' to 'CCP Inc.': A New Paradigm for Chinese State Capitalism." *China Leadership Monitor* 66: December 1.

British Broadcasting Corporation. 2020. "Ren Zhiqiang: Outspoken Ex-Real Estate Tycoon Gets 18 Years Jail." September 22. www.bbc.com/news/world-asia-china-54245327.

2021. "Outspoken Billionaire Sun Dawu Jailed for 18 Years in China." July 29. www.bbc.co.uk/news/world-asia-china-58007515.

Brownlee, Jason. 2007. *Authoritarianism in an Age of Democratization*. New York: Cambridge University Press.

Bueno de Mesquita, Bruce, Alastair Smith, Randolph M. Siverson, and James D. Morrow. 2003. *The Logic of Political Survival*. Cambridge, MA: MIT Press.

Bunce, Valerie J. 1981. *Do New Leaders Make a Difference? Executive Succession and Public Policy under Capitalism and Socialism*. Princeton, NJ: Princeton University Press.

Bunce, Valerie J. and Sharon L. Wolchik. 2011. *Defeating Authoritarian Leaders in Postcommunist Countries*. New York: Cambridge University Press.

Burns, John P. 1990. "The Structure of Communist Party Control in Hong Kong." *Asian Survey* 30 (8): 748–765.

2022. "The Chinese Communist Party in Hong Kong." Riyadh: King Faisal Center for Research and Islamic Studies Special Report.

Byler, Darren. 2022. *Terror Capitalism: Uyghur Dispossession and Masculinity in a Chinese City*. Durham, NC: Duke University Press.

Cai, Yongshun. 2010. *Collective Resistance in China: Why Popular Protests Succeed or Fail*. Stanford, CA: Stanford University Press.

Cai, Yongshun and Chih-Jou Jay Chen. 2022. *State and Social Protests in China*. Cambridge: Cambridge University Press.

Cantoni, Davide, Yuyu Chen, David Y. Yang, Noam Yuchtman, and Y. Jane Zhang. 2017. "Curriculum and Ideology." *Journal of Political Economy* 125 (2): 338–392.

Carothers, Christopher. 2022. *Corruption Control in Authoritarian Regimes: Lessons from East Asia*. New York: Cambridge University Press.

Chang, Gordon G. 2001. *The Coming Collapse of China*. New York: Random House.

Cheek, Timothy, Klaus Mühlhahn, and Hans van de Ven, eds. 2021. *The Chinese Communist Party: A Century in Ten Lives*. New York: Cambridge University Press.

Chen, Calvin. 2008. *Some Assembly Required: Work, Community, and Politics in China's Rural Enterprises*. Cambridge, MA: Harvard University Asia Center.

Chen, Chih-Jou Jay and Yongshun Cai. 2021. "Upward Targeting and Social Protest in China." *Journal of Contemporary China* 30 (130): 511–525.

Chen, Hao and Meg Rithmire. 2020. "The Rise of the Investor State: State Capital in the Chinese Economy." *Studies in Comparative International Development* 55 (3): 257–277.

Chen Huadong. 2013. "Wangluo yuyan baquan yujing xia daxuesheng jiaoyu guanli gongzuo de tiaozhan yu sikao." *Sixiang Lilun Jiaoyu* 7: 72–76, 81.

Chen, Huirong and Sheena Chestnut Greitens. 2022. "Information Capacity and Social Order: The Local Politics of Information Integration in China." *Governance* 35 (2): 497–523.

Chen, Xi. 2012. *Social Protest and Contentious Authoritarianism in China.* New York: Cambridge University Press.

China NGO Project. 2022. "The Major Questions about China's Foreign NGO Law Are Now Settled: And so Farewell from the China NGO Project." August 8. www.chinafile.com.

Cook, Linda J. 1993. *The Soviet Social Contract and Why It Failed: Welfare Policy and Workers' Politics from Brezhnev to Yeltsin.* Cambridge, MA: Harvard University Press.

Cook, Linda J. and Martin K. Dimitrov. 2017. "The Social Contract Revisited: Evidence from Communist and State Capitalist Economies." *Europe-Asia Studies* 69 (1): 8–26.

Cui Jianmin and Chen Dongping, eds. 2016. *Dang de jianshe yanjiu baogao 2016.* Beijing: Shehui Kexue Wenxian Chubanshe.

Cui Yadong. 2013. *Quntixing shijian yingji guanli yu shehui zhili: Weng'an zhiluan dao Weng'an zhizhi.* Beijing: Zhonggong Zhongyang Dangxiao Chubanshe.

Cunningham, Edward, Tony Saich, and Jesse Turiel. 2020. "Understanding CCP Resilience: Surveying Chinese Public Opinion through Time." Policy Brief, Harvard Kennedy School Ash Center.

Dallin, Alexander and George W. Breslauer. 1970. *Political Terror in Communist Systems.* Stanford, CA: Stanford University Press.

Deutsche Welle. 2022. "Lu Shaye tan baizhi yundong: 'Ye shi yanse geming.'" December 15. www.dw.com/zh/a-64126605.

Dickson, Bruce J. 1997. *Democratization in China and Taiwan: The Adaptability of Leninist Parties.* New York: Clarendon Press.

2003. *Red Capitalists in China: The Party, Private Entrepreneurs, and Prospects for Political Change.* New York: Cambridge University Press.

2008. *Wealth into Power: The Communist Party's Embrace of China's Private Sector.* New York: Cambridge University Press.

2016. *The Dictator's Dilemma: The Chinese Communist Party's Strategy for Survival.* New York: Oxford University Press.

2021. *The Party and the People: Chinese Politics in the 21st Century.* Princeton, NJ: Princeton University Press.

Dillon, Nara. 2015. *Radical Inequalities: China's Revolutionary Welfare State in Comparative Perspective.* Cambridge, MA: Harvard University Asia Center.

Dimitrov, Martin K. 2009. *Piracy and the State: The Politics of Intellectual Property Rights in China*. New York: Cambridge University Press.

ed. 2013. *Why Communism Did Not Collapse: Understanding Authoritarian Regime Resilience in Asia and Europe*. New York: Cambridge University Press.

2016. "Structural Preconditions for the Rise of the Rule of Law in China." *Journal of Chinese Governance* 1 (3): 470–487.

2017. "Kémekből oligarchák." *Arc és Álarc* (Fall–Winter): 9–34.

2018. *Politicheskata logika na sotsialististicheskoto potreblenie*. Sofia: Ciela.

2019. "European Lessons for China: Tiananmen 1989 and Beyond." In Piotr H. Kosicki and Kyrill Kunakhovich, eds., *The Long 1989: Decades of Global Revolution*, 61–88. New York: Central European University Press.

2023. *Dictatorship and Information: Authoritarian Regime Resilience in Communist Europe and China*. New York: Oxford University Press.

2024. "Why Size Matters: The Origins and Effects of Variation in Party Size in Revolutionary and Nonrevolutionary Regimes." In Natasha Lindstaedt and Joroen Van den Bosch, eds., *Research Handbook on Authoritarianism*, 96–110. Cheltenham: Edward Elgar Publishing.

Dimitrov, Martin K. and Zhu Zhang. 2021. "The Political Economy of Stability Maintenance under Xi Jinping." In Lowell Dittmer, ed., *China's Political Economy in the Xi Jinping Epoch: Domestic and Global Dimensions*, 127–162. Singapore: World Scientific.

Ding, Iza. 2020. "Performative Governance." *World Politics* 72 (4): 525–556.

2022. *The Performative State: Public Scrutiny and Environmental Governance in China*. Ithaca, NY: Cornell University Press.

Ding Jun and Rao Junni. 2021. "Guoxue jingdian yu daxuesheng sixiang zhengzhi jiaoyi de ronghe." *Xinan Linye Daxue Xuebao* 5 (2): 107–110.

Ding Yi. 2021. "Out-of-Favor Jack Ma Tops Forbes China Philanthropy List." *Caixin Global*, July 26. www.caixinglobal.com/2021-07-26/out-of-favor-jack-ma-tops-forbes-china-philanthropy-list-with-494-million-in-donations-101745791.html .

Distelhortst, Greg and Yue Hou. 2017. "Constituency Service under Non-Democratic Rule: Evidence from China." *Journal of Politics* 79 (3): 1024–1040.

Dragostinova, Theodora K. 2021. *The Cold War from the Margins: A Small Socialist State on the Global Cultural Scene*. Ithaca, NY: Cornell University Press.

Duckett, Jane. 2011. *The Chinese State's Retreat from Health: Policy and the Politics of Retrenchment*. London: Routledge.

The Economist. 2022. "Alibaba and the 40 Officials." May 7. www.economist .com/business/can-chinese-big-tech-learn-to-love-big-brother/21809084.

2023. "China Tells Its Citizens to Be on the Lookout for Spies." September 21. www.economist.com/china/2023/09/21/china-tells-its-citizens-to-be-on-the-lookout-for-spies.

Ekiert, Grzegorz. 1996. *The State against Society: Political Crises and Their Aftermath in East Central Europe.* Princeton, NJ: Princeton University Press.

Elfstrom, Isaac Manfred. 2019. "Two Steps Forward, One Step Back: Chinese Reactions to Labor Unrest." *The China Quarterly* 240: 855–879.

2021. *Workers and Change in China: Resistance, Repression, Responsiveness.* New York: Cambridge University Press.

Fewsmith, Joseph. 2021. *Rethinking Chinese Politics.* New York: Cambridge University Press.

Five-Year Planning Outline for Advancing the Sinification of Christianity 2018–2022. 2017. Beijing: National Committee of the Christian Three-Self Movement.

Five-Year Planning Outline for Persisting in the Sinification of Islam 2018–2022. 2017. Beijing: China Islamic Association.

Forsythe, Michael. 2015. "Wang Jianlin, A Billionaire at the Intersection of Business and Power in China." *The New York Times*, April 28. www.nytimes.com/2015/04/29/world/asia/wang-jianlin-abillionaire-at-the-intersection-of-business-and-power-in-china.html

Frazier, Mark W. 2010. *Socialist Insecurity: Pensions and the Politics of Uneven Development in China.* Ithaca, NY: Cornell University Press.

Freedom House. 2024. *Freedom in the World 2024.* Washington, DC: Freedom House.

Freeland, Chrystia. 2000. *Sale of the Century: The Inside Story of the Second Russian Republic.* New York: Crown Business.

Friedrich, Carl J. and Zbigniew Brzezinski. 1965. *Totalitarian Dictatorship and Autocracy.* New York: Praeger.

Frye, Timothy. 2006. "Original Sin, Good Works, and Property Rights in Russia." *World Politics* 58 (4): 479–504.

Fu, Diana. 2018. *Mobilizing Without the Masses: Control and Contention in China.* New York: Cambridge University Press.

Fukuyama, Francis. 1989. "The End of History?" *The National Interest* 16 (Summer): 3–18.

Fukuyama, Francis. 1992. *The End of History and the Last Man.* New York: Free Press.

Fulbrook, Mary. 2005. *The People's State: East German Society from Hitler to Honecker*. New Haven, CT: Yale University Press.

Fürst, Rudolf. 2021. "Cultivating the Art of Anxiety: Securitising Culture in China." *China Report* 57 (4): 433–450.

Gaige Neican. 2012. No. 11: 1–11.

2014a. No. 13: 2–20.

2014b. No. 27: 27–33.

Gallagher, Mary E. 2005. *Contagious Capitalism: Globalization and the Politics of Labor in China*. Princeton, NJ: Princeton University Press.

2017. *Authoritarian Legality in China: Law, Workers, and the State*. New York: Cambridge University Press.

Gallagher, Mary E. and Blake Miller. 2021. "Who Not What: The Logic of China's Information Control Strategy." *The China Quarterly* 248: 1011–1036.

Gandhi, Jennifer. 2008. *Political Institutions under Dictatorship*. New York: Cambridge University Press.

Ganev, Venelin I. 2007. *Preying on the State: The Transformation of Bulgaria after 1989*. Ithaca, NY: Cornell University Press.

Gansu Sheng Difang Shizhi Bangongshi. 2020. *Gansu nianjian 2020*. Lanzhou: Gansu Minzu Chubanshe.

Gao, Jie. 2016. "'Bypass the Lying Mouths': How Does the CCP Tackle Information Distortion at Local Levels?" *The China Quarterly* 228: 950–969.

Gao, Qin. 2010. "Redistributive Nature of the Chinese Social Benefit System: Progressive or Regressive?" *The China Quarterly* 201: 1–19.

García Herrero, Alicia. 2021 "What is Behind China's Dual Circulation Strategy." *China Leadership Monitor* 69: September 1.

Geddes, Barbara, Joseph Wright, and Erica Frantz. 2018. *How Dictatorships Work*. New York: Cambridge University Press.

Geddes, Thomas des Garets. 2020. "As Hong Kong Rebels, Why Is Macau So Quiet?" *MERICS Analysis*, January 21. https://merics.org/en/comment/hong-kong-rebels-why-macau-so-quiet.

Gilley, Bruce. 2004. *China's Democratic Future: How It Will Happen and Where It Will Lead*. New York: Columbia University Press.

Göbel, Christian. 2019. "Social Unrest in China: A Bird's Eye View." In Teresa Wright, ed., *Handbook of Protest and Resistance in China*, 27–45. Cheltenham: Edward Elgar.

Groot, Gerry. 2004. *Managing Transitions: The Chinese Communist Party, United Front Work, Corporatism, and Hegemony*. New York: Routledge.

Guan, Guihai. 2010. "The Influence of the Collapse of the Soviet Union on Chinese Political Choices." In Thomas P. Bernstein and Hua-yu Li, eds.,

China Learns from the Soviet Union, 1949–Present, 505–515. Lanham, MD: Lexington Books

Guangdong Sheng Renmin Zhengfu. 2021. *Guangdong nianjian 2021*. Guangzhou: Yachang Wenhua Youxian Gongsi.

Gueorguiev, Dimitar D. 2021. *Retrofitting Leninism: Participation Without Democracy in China*. New York: Oxford University Press.

Gueorguiev, Dimitar D. and Edmund J. Malesky. 2019. "Consultation and Selective Censorship in China." *Journal of Politics* 81 (4): 1539–1545.

Guoji Guanxi Xueyuan Guoji Zhanlüe yu Anquan Yanjiu Zhongxin. 2010. *2009 nian Zhongguo guojia anquan gailan*. Beijing: Shishi Chubanshe.

Guojia Anquan Bu. 1987. "Guojia anquan jiguan ji qi gongzuo." Beijing: Guojia Anquan Bu Bangongting.

 1989. "1987 nian de guojia anquan gongzuo." Beijing: Guojia Anquan Bu Bangongting.

 1990a. "1988 nian de guojia anquan gongzuo." Beijing: Guojia Anquan Bu Bangongting.

 1990b. "1989 nian de guojia anquan gongzuo." Beijing: Guojia Anquan Bu Bangongting.

 1991. "1990 nian de guojia anquan gongzuo." Beijing: Guojia Anquan Bu Bangongting.

Guojia Wenhua Anquan Zhishi Baiwen Bianxie Zu. 2022. *Guojia wenhua anquan zhishi baiwen*. Beijing: Renmin Chubanshe.

Guowuyuan Fazhan Yanjiu Zhongxin. 2004. *Guoji yisilan jiduan shili dui Xinjiang de yingxiang*. Beijing: Guowuyuan Fazhan Yanjiu Zhongxin.

Hainan Sheng Renmin Zhengfu. 2020. *Hainan nianjian 2020*. Xi'an: Sanqin Chubanshe.

Han Yuan. 2016. *Zhongguo wenhua anquan pinglun*. Beijing: Shehui Kexue Wenxian Chubanshe.

Hauslohner, Peter. 1987. "Gorbachev's Social Contract." *Soviet Economy* 3 (1): 54–89.

Havel, Václav. 1979. *Moc bezmocných*. London: Londýnské listy.

He Hua and Hu Jianghua. 2022. "Sulian jieti de wenhua anquan yinsu shenshi ji dui woguo wenhua anquan de qishi." *Shehui Kexue Dongtai*, no. 6: 23–29.

He Xinsheng, Tian Miao, and Song Tushun. 2020. "Zhongguo wenhua ruanshili zai Xiongyali chuanbo yanjiu." *Huabei Ligong Daxue Xuebao* 20 (4): 143–149.

Heilmann, Sebastian. 2011. "Experience First, Laws Later." In Jean C. Oi, ed., *Going Private in China*, 95–118. Stanford, CA: Asia-Pacific Research Center.

Heilmann, Sebastian and Elizabeth J. Perry, eds. 2011. *Mao's Invisible Hand: The Political Foundations of Adaptive Governance in China.* Cambridge, MA: Harvard University Press.

Heurlin, Christopher. 2016. *Responsive Authoritarianism in China: Land, Protests, and Policymaking.* New York: Cambridge University Press.

Hoffman, David E. 2002. *The Oligarchs: Wealth and Power in the New Russia.* Oxford: Public Affairs.

Holbig, Heike. 2004. "The Party and Private Entrepreneurs in the PRC." In Kjeld Erik Brødsgaard and Zheng Yongnian, eds., *Bringing the Party Back In: How China Is Governed*, 239–267. Singapore: Eastern Universities Press.

——— 2020. "Be Water, My Friend: Hong Kong's 2019 Anti-Extradition Protests." *International Journal of Sociology* 50 (4): 325–337.

Holbig, Heike and Bertram Lang. 2022. "China's Overseas NGO Law and the Future of International Civil Society." *Journal of Contemporary Asia* 52 (4): 574–601.

Hoover Institution. 2004. *Cold War Broadcasting Impact.* Stanford, CA: Hoover Institution.

Hou, Yue. 2019. *The Private Sector in Public Office: Selective Property Rights in China.* New York: Cambridge University Press.

Howlett, Zachary M. 2021. *Meritocracy and Its Discontents: Anxiety and the National College Entrance Exam in China.* Ithaca, NY: Cornell University Press.

Hsu, Jennifer Y. J. 2017. *State of Exchange: Migrant NGOs and the Chinese Government.* Vancouver: UBC Press.

Hsu, Szu-chien, Kellee S. Tsai, and Chun-chih Chang, eds. 2021. *Evolutionary Governance in China: State-Society Relations under Authoritarianism.* Cambridge, MA: Harvard University Asia Center.

Hu, Jieren, Peng Zeng, and Tong Wu. 2022. "How Are 'Red Social Workers' Trained? Party-Building Absorption of Society in China." *China Review* 22 (3): 297–323.

Huang, Jingyang and Kellee S. Tsai. 2021. "Upgrading Big Brother: Local Strategic Adaptations in China's Security Industry." *Studies in Comparative International Development* 56 (4): 560–587.

Huang, Xian. 2015. "Four Worlds of Welfare: Understanding Subnational Variation in Chinese Social Health Insurance." *The China Quarterly* 222: 449–474.

——— 2020. *Social Protection under Authoritarianism: Health Politics and Policy in China.* New York: Oxford University Press.

Huang, Yasheng. 2008. *Capitalism with Chinese Characteristics: Entrepreneurship and the State*. New York: Cambridge University Press.

Hubei Sheng Renmin Zhengfu. 2020. *Hubei nianjian 2020*. Wuhan: Hubei Nianjian She.

Hunan Sheng Renmin Zhengfu. 2020. *Hunan nianjian 2020*. Changsha: Hunan Sheng Meiruhua Caise Yinshua Youxian Gongsi.

Huntington, Samuel P. 1968. *Political Order in Changing Societies*. New Haven, CT: Yale University Press.

Hurst, William. 2009. *The Chinese Worker after Socialism*. Cambridge: Cambridge University Press.

Introvigne, Massimo. 2022. "'White Is Also a Color': CCP Blames Protests on American Conspiracy." *Bitter Winter*. bitterwinter.org/ccp-blames-pro tests-on-american-conspiracy/

Jancar-Webster, Barbara. 1998. "Environmental Movement and Social Change in the Transition Countries." *Environmental Politics* 7 (1): 69–90.

Jee, Haemin. 2022. "Credit for Compliance: How Institutional Proliferation Establishes Control in China." Working Paper.

Jiang Hui. 2016. "Ouzhou yuyan baquan shi houzhimin lilun de linghun." *Wenyi Lilun yu Piping*, no. 1: 75–81.

Jing, Peitong and Karrie J. Koesel. 2024. "Securitization through Sinicization: Church & State in Contemporary China." *Politics and Religion*, DOI: 10.1017/S1755048323000329.

Johnson, Matthew D. 2017. "Securitizing Culture in Post-Deng China: An Evolving National Strategic Paradigm, 1994–2014." *Propaganda in the World and Local Conflicts* 4 (1): 62–80.

Johnston, Timothy D. 1981. "Contrasting Approaches to a Theory of Learning." *The Behavioral and Brain Sciences* 4 (1): 125–173.

Keister, Lisa A. 2000. *Chinese Business Groups: The Structure and Impact of Interfirm Relations during Economic Development*. New York: Oxford University Press.

Kim, Jieun and Peter Lorentzen. 2023. "China's Blacklists." Working Paper.

King, Gary, Jennifer Pan, and Margaret E. Roberts. 2013. "How Censorship in China Allows Government Criticism but Silences Collective Expression." *American Political Science Review* 107 (2): 326–343.

2017. "How the Chinese Government Fabricates Social Media Posts for Strategic Distraction, Not Engaged Argument." *American Political Science Review* 111 (3): 484–501.

Klebnikov, Paul. 2000. *Godfather of the Kremlin: Boris Berezovsky and the Looting of Russia*. New York: Harcourt.

Klotzbücher, Sascha, Peter Lässig, Qin Jiangmei, and Susanne Weigelin-Schwiedrzik. 2010. "What Is New in the 'New Rural Co-operative Medical System'? An Assessment of One Kazak County of the Xinjiang Uyghur Autonomous Region." *The China Quarterly* 201: 38–57.

Koesel, Karrie J. 2014. *Religion and Authoritarianism: Cooperation Conflict, and the Consequences*. New York: Cambridge University Press.

2020. "Legitimacy, Resilience, and Political Education in Russia and China: Learning to Be Loyal." In Karrie J. Koesel, Valerie J. Bunce, and Jessica Chen Weiss, eds., *Citizens and the State in Authoritarian Regimes: Comparing China and Russia*, 250–278. New York: Oxford University Press.

Koesel, Karrie J. and Valerie J. Bunce. 2013. "Diffusion-Proofing: Russian and Chinese Responses to Waves of Popular Mobilizations against Authoritarian Rulers." *Perspectives on Politics* 11 (3): 753–768.

Kornai, János. 1980. *Economics of Shortage*. Amsterdam: Elsevier.

Koss, Daniel. 2021. "Party Building as Institutional Bricolage: Asserting Authority at the Business Frontier." *The China Quarterly* 248 (S1): 222–243.

Kubik, Jan. 1994. *The Power of Symbols against the Symbols of Power: The Rise of Solidarity and the Fall of State Socialism in Poland*. University Park, PA: Pennsylvania State University Press.

Kuran, Timur. 1991. "Now out of Never: The Element of Surprise in the East European Revolution of 1989." *World Politics* 44 (1): 7–48.

Kurlantzick, Joshua. 2016. *State Capitalism: How the Return of Statism Is Transforming the World*. New York: Oxford University Press.

Lee, Ching Kwan and Yonghong Zhang. 2013. "The Power of Instability: Unraveling the Microfoundations of Bargained Authoritarianism in China." *American Journal of Sociology* 118 (6): 1475–1508.

Leibold, James. 2020. "Surveillance in China's Xinjiang Region: Ethnic Sorting, Coercion, and Inducement." *Journal of Contemporary China* 29 (121): 46–60.

Levitsky, Steven R. and Lucan A. Way. 2022. *Revolution and Dictatorship: The Violent Origins of Durable Authoritarianism*. Princeton, NJ: Princeton University Press.

Li, Lianjiang. 2016. "Reassessing Trust in the Central Government: Evidence from Five National Surveys." *The China Quarterly* 225: 100–121.

Li Peilin, Chen Guangjin, and Wang Chunguang. 2020. *Zhongguo shehui xingshi fenxi yu yuce 2020*. Beijing: Shehui Kexue Wenxian Chubanshe.

Li Peilin, Chen Guangjin, and Zhang Yi, eds. 2015. *Zhongguo shehui xingshi fenxi yu yuce 2016*. Beijing: Shehui Kexue Wenxian Chubanshe.

2019. *Zhongguo shehui xingshi fenxi yu yuce 2019*. Beijing: Shehui Kexue Wenxian Chubanshe.

Li, Yao. 2019. *Playing by the Informal Rules: Why the Chinese Regime Remains Stable Despite Rising Protests*. New York: Cambridge University Press.

Li Yingjun. 2016. "'Pushi jiazhi' chongji xia de gaoxiao yishi xingtai anquan yanjiu." MA Thesis, School of Marxism, Shanxi University of Finance and Economics.

Li Zhonghua. 2007. "Guoxue, guoxue re yu wenhua rentong." *Beijing Xingzheng Xueyuan Xuebao*, no. 3: 96–101.

Li Zonggui. 2008. "Guoxue yu shidai jingshen." *Xueshu Yanjiu*, no. 3: 21–32.

Lin Weiye and Liu Hanmin. 2008. *Gong'an jiguan yingdui quntixing shijian shiwu yu celüe*. Beijing: Zhongguo Renmin Gong'an Daxue Chubanshe.

Lingdao Canyue. 2013. No. 20: 34–37.

2014. No. 29: 23–26.

Liu, Jun. 2013. "Mobile Communication, Popular Protests and Citizenship in China." *Modern Asian Studies* 47 (3): 995–1018.

Liu Meimei. 2020. "Qiantan 'guoxue re' zhong cunzai de wenti ji yingdui." *Hanzi Wenhua*, no. 2: 153–155.

Liu Yanping. 2013. "Quanqiuhua beijing xia Riben donghua zhong de wenhua chuanbo he wenhua shentou." MA Thesis, School of Journalism and Communication, Zhengzhou University.

Loh, Christine. 2018. *Underground Front: The Chinese Communist Party in Hong Kong*. 2nd ed. Hong Kong: Hong Kong University Press.

Lohmann, Susanne. 1994. "The Dynamics of Informational Cascades: The Monday Demonstrations in Leipzig, East Germany, 1989–91." *World Politics* 47 (1): 42–101.

Lorentzen, Peter. 2013. "Regularizing Rioting: Permitting Public Protest in an Authoritarian Regime." *Quarterly Journal of Political Science* 8 (2): 127–158.

2017. "Designing Contentious Politics in Post-1989 China." *Modern China* 43 (5): 459–493.

Lu Jianyou. 2020. "Xifang wangluo waijiao yu gaoxiao yishi xingtai anquan wenti chuyi." *Gaoxiao Gongqingtuan Yanjiu*, no. 11–12: 28–32.

Lu Xia and Zhou Yong. 2020. "Ziben zhuyi quanqiuhua beijing xia yingyu yuyan baquan xianxiang tanxi." *Chongqing Ligong Daxue Xuebao (Shehui Kexue)* 34 (10): 114–122.

Magaloni, Beatriz. 2006. *Voting for Autocracy: Hegemonic Party Survival and its Demise in Mexico*. New York: Cambridge University Press.

Manion, Melanie. 1993. *Retirement of Revolutionaries in China: Public Policies, Social Norms, Private Interests*. Princeton, NJ: Princeton University Press.

Markus, Stanislav. 2015. *Property, Predation, and Protection: Piranha Capitalism in Russia and Ukraine*. New York: Cambridge University Press.

Martin, Peter. 2021. *China's Civilian Army: The Making of Wolf Warrior Diplomacy*. New York: Oxford University Press.

Mattingly, Daniel C. 2020. *The Art of Political Control in China*. New York: Cambridge University Press.

McGregor, Richard. 2010. *The Party: The Secret World of China's Communist Rulers*. New York: Harper.

Measures for the Administration of Religious Groups. 2019. Beijing: State Administration for Religious Affairs.

Meng, Anne. 2020. *Constraining Dictatorship: From Personalized Rule to Institutionalized Regimes*. New York: Cambridge University Press.

Mertha, Andrew C. 2005. *The Politics of Piracy: Intellectual Property in Contemporary China*. Ithaca, NY: Cornell University Press.

Millar, James R. 1985. "The Little Deal: Brezhnev's Contribution to Acquisitive Socialism." *Slavic Review* 44 (4): 694–706.

Miller, Blake. 2018. "Delegated Dictatorship: Examining the State and Market Forces Behind Information Control in China." PhD Dissertation, Department of Political Science, University of Michigan.

Mulvenon, James. 2001. *Soldiers of Fortune: The Rise and Fall of the Military–Business Complex, 1978–1998*. Armonk, NY: M. E. Sharpe.

Nathan, Andrew. 2003. "China's Changing of the Guard: Authoritarian Resilience." *Journal of Democracy* 14 (1): 6–17.

Naughton, Barry. 1995. *Growing Out of the Plan: Chinese Economic Reform, 1978–1983*. New York: Cambridge University Press.

2020. "Grand Steerage." In Thomas Fingar and Jean C. Oi, eds., *Fateful Decisions: Choices That Will Shape China's Future*, 51–81. Stanford, CA: Stanford University Press.

Naughton, Barry and Kellee S. Tsai, eds. 2015. *State Capitalism, Institutional Adaptation, and the Chinese Miracle*. New York: Cambridge University Press.

Neibu Canyue. 1991. No. 40.

2013a. No. 25: 43–48.

2013b. No. 28: 3–13.

Nepstad, Sharon. 2011. *Nonviolent Revolutions: Civil Resistance in the Late 20th Century*. New York: Oxford University Press.

Ningxia Difangzhi Bianshen Weiyuanhui. 2019. *Ningxia nianjian 2019*. Beijing: Fangzhi Chubanshe.

NSC 68. 1950. *A Report to the National Security Council by the Executive Secretary on United States Objectives and Programs for National Security*. Washington, DC: National Security Council, April 14.

O'Brien, Kevin J. and Lianjiang Li. 2006. *Rightful Resistance in Rural China*. New York: Cambridge University Press.

Oi, Jean C. 1985. "Communism and Clientelism: Rural Politics in China." *World Politics* 37 (2): 238–266.

1999. *Rural China Takes Off: Institutional Foundations of Economic Reform*. Berkeley, CA: University of California Press.

ed. 2011. *Going Private in China*. Stanford, CA: Asia-Pacific Research Center.

Oi, Jean C. and Steven M. Goldstein, eds. 2018. *Zouping Revisited: Adaptive Governance in a Chinese County*. Stanford, CA: Stanford University Press.

Ong, Lynette. 2022. *Outsourcing Repression: Everyday State Power in Contemporary China*. New York: Oxford University Press.

Orenstein, Mitchell A. 2001. *Out of the Red: Building Capitalism and Democracy in Postcommunist Europe*. Ann Arbor, MI: University of Michigan Press.

Ost, David. 2006. *The Defeat of Solidarity: Anger and Politics in Postcommunist Europe*. Ithaca, NY: Cornell University Press.

Palmer, David A. 2007. *Qigong Fever: Body, Science, and Utopia in China*. New York: Columbia University Press.

Pan, Jennifer. 2020. *Welfare for Autocrats: How Social Assistance in China Cares for Its Rulers*. New York: Oxford University Press.

Pan, Jennifer and Kaiping Chen. 2018. "Concealing Corruption: How Chinese Officials Distort Upward Reporting of Online Grievances." *American Political Science Review* 112 (3): 602–620.

Pan Xinzhe and Liu Aidi. 2016. "Wenhua zixin de lilun jichu yu shijian yaoqiu." *Makesi Zhuyi Yanjiu*, no. 11: 64–73.

Pearson, Margaret, Meg Rithmire, and Kellee S. Tsai. 2020. "Party-State Capitalism in China." Harvard Business School Working Paper 21–065.

2023. *The State and Capitalism in China*. Cambridge: Cambridge University Press.

Pei, Minxin. 2006. *China's Trapped Transition: The Limits of Developmental Autocracy*. Cambridge, MA: Harvard University Press.

Pepper, Suzanne. 2021. "Out of the Shadows: How China's Communist Party Is Now Claiming Credit for the Hong Kong Success Story." *Hong Kong Free Press*, July 11. https://hongkongfp.com/2021/07/11/how-chinas-commun ist-party-is-now-claiming-credit-for-the-hong-kong-success-story/.

Perry, Elizabeth J. 2002. *Challenging the Mandate of Heaven: Social Protest and State Power in China*. Armonk, NY: M. E. Sharpe.

2020. "Educated Acquiescence: How Academia Sustains Authoritarianism in China." *Theory and Society* 49 (5): 1–22.

Qi Weiping. 2016. "Wenhua zixin de shizhi yu yiyi." *Zhongyuan Wenhua Yanjiu*, no. 5: 22–28.

Qian, Isabelle, Muyi Xiao, Paul Mozur, and Alexander Cardia. 2022. "China's Expanding Surveillance State." *The New York Times*, June 21. www .nytimes.com/2022/06/21/world/asia/china-surveillance-investigation .html.

Qin Weidong. 1990. *Xizang wenti beiwanglu*. Lanzhou: Lanzhou Junqu Zhengzhibu Lianluobu.

Qinghai Sheng Difangzhi Bianzuan Weiyuanhui. 2019. *Qinghai nianjian 2019*. Xining: Qinghai Nianjian She.

Renmin Ribao. 2013. "Jianjue daji 'sangu shili.'" July 1.

Renmin Xinfang. 1989a. No. 10: 2.

1989b. No. 10: 3–8.

1989c. No. 11: 2–4.

1990. No. 2: 2–3.

2000a. No. 3: 3.

2000b. No. 7: 16.

2010. No. 2 (313): 6.

Reny, Marie-Eve. 2018. *Authoritarian Containment: Public Security Bureaus and Protestant Churches in Urban China*. New York: Oxford University Press.

Renzhen Luose, Xie Gangzheng, and Chen Zhichun. 2001. *Suowei 'Xizang wenti' de lishi yu xianzhuang*. [Sichuan]: Sichuan Zangxue Yanjiusuo.

Repnikova, Maria. 2022. *Chinese Soft Power*. New York: Cambridge University Press.

Rithmire, Meg. 2023. *Precarious Ties: Business and the State in Authoritarian Asia*. New York: Oxford University Press.

Rithmire, Meg and Hao Chen. 2021. "The Emergence of Mafia-like Business Systems in China." *The China Quarterly* 248: 1037–1058.

Roberts, Margaret E. 2018. *Censored: Distraction and Diversion Inside China's Great Wall*. Princeton, NJ: Princeton University Press.

Roberts, Sean R. 2020. *The War on the Uyghurs: China's Campaign against a Muslim Minority*. Princeton, NJ: Princeton University Press.

Rowen, Henry. 1996. "The Short March: China's Road to Democracy." *The National Interest* 45 (Fall): 61–70.

Ruan, Lotus, Masashi Crete-Nishihata, Jeffrey Knockel, Ruohan Xiong, and Jakub Dalek. 2021. "The Intermingling of State and Private Companies: Analysing Censorship of the 19th National Communist Party Congress on WeChat." *The China Quarterly* 246: 497–526.

Saich, Tony. 2000. "Negotiating the State: The Development of Social Organizations in China." *The China Quarterly* 161: 121–141.

2021. *From Rebel to Ruler: One Hundred Years of the Chinese Communist Party*. Cambridge, MA: Harvard University Press.

Scoggins, Suzanne E. 2021. *Policing China: Street-Level Cops in the Shadow of Protest*. Ithaca, NY: Cornell University Press.

Shambaugh, David. 2008. *China's Communist Party: Atrophy and Adaptation*. Washington, DC: Woodrow Wilson Center Press.

2021. *China's Leaders: From Mao to Now*. Cambridge, MA: Polity.

Shanghai Municipal Archives. 1965. Document B180-1-41-15.

Shih, Victor. 2022. *Coalitions of the Weak: Elite Politics in China from Mao's Stratagem to the Rise of Xi*. New York: Cambridge University Press.

Shirk, Susan L. 2007. *China: Fragile Superpower*. New York: Oxford University Press.

2023. *Overreach: How China Derailed Its Peaceful Rise*. New York: Oxford University Press.

Shum, Desmond. 2021. *Red Roulette: An Insider's Story of Wealth, Power, Corruption, and Vengeance in Today's China*. New York: Scribner.

Sichuan Sheng Zhengfu. 2019. *Sichuan nianjian 2019*. Chengdu: Sichuan Nianjian She.

Slater, Dan and Joseph Wong. 2022. *From Development to Democracy: The Transformations of Modern Asia*. Princeton, NJ: Princeton University Press.

Smith, Benjamin. 2005. "Life of the Party: The Origins of Regime Breakdown and Persistence under Single-Party Rule." *World Politics* 57 (3): 421–451.

Solinger, Dorothy. 2022. *Poverty and Pacification: The Chinese State Abandons the Old Working Class*. Lanham, MD: Rowman & Littlefield.

Spires, Anthony J. 2011 "Contingent Symbiosis and Civil Society in an Authoritarian State: Understanding the Survival of China's Grassroots NGOs." *American Journal of Sociology* 117 (1): 1–45.

Steinfeld, Edward S. 2010. *Playing Our Game: Why China's Rise Doesn't Threaten the West*. New York: Oxford University Press.

Sun Liping. 2011. "Shehui shixu shi dangxia de yanjun tiaozhan." *Jingji Guancha Bao*, February 25.

Sun, Yu. 2023. "Millions Drop Out of China's State Health Insurance System." *Financial Times*, December 10.

Svolik, Milan W. 2012. *The Politics of Authoritarian Rule*. New York: Cambridge University Press.

Takeuchi, Hiroki. 2014. *Tax Reform in Rural China: Revenue, Resistance, and Authoritarian Rule*. New York: Cambridge University Press.

Tang, Wenfang and Qing Yang. 2008. "The Chinese Urban Caste System in Transition." *The China Quarterly* 196: 759–779.

Tao Jianjie and Yin Ziyi. 2021. "Zhongguo wenhua ruanshili de shizheng pinggu yu moni yuce." *Weilai Chuanbo* 28 (4): 14–23.

Teets, Jessica C. 2014. *Civil Society under Authoritarianism: The China Model.* New York: Cambridge University Press.

Thomas, Daniel C. 2001. *The Helsinki Effect: International Norms, Human Rights, and the Demise of Communism.* Princeton, NJ: Princeton University Press.

Tian Xianhong. 2012. "Yishi xingtai zhuanxing yu xinfang zhuli de lunli kunjing." *Zhanlüe yu Guanli: Neibu Ban*, nos. 5–6: 39–54.

Tianjin tongzhi: Xinfang zhi. 1997. Tianjin: Tianjin Shehui Kexueyuan Chubanshe.

Tismaneanu, Vladimir. 2013. "Ideological Erosion and the Breakdown of Communist Regimes." In Martin K. Dimitrov, ed., *Why Communism Did Not Collapse: Understanding Authoritarian Regime Resilience in Asia and Europe*, 67–98. New York: Cambridge University Press.

Tong, James W. 2009. *Revenge of the Forbidden City: The Suppression of the Falungong in China, 1999–2005.* New York: Oxford University Press.

Tong, Yanqi and Shaohua Lei. 2014. *Social Protest in Contemporary China, 2003–2010: Transitional Pains and Regime Legitimacy.* New York: Routledge.

Tsai, Kellee S. 2007. *Capitalism Without Democracy: The Private Sector in Contemporary China.* Ithaca, NY: Cornell University Press.

Tsai, Wen-Hsuan, Hsin-Hsien Wang, and Ruihua Lin. 2021. "Hobbling Big Brother: Top-Level Design and Local Discretion in China's Social Credit System." *The China Journal.* 86: 1–20.

Tsvetanski, Stoian. 1988. *Organizatsionno razvitie na BKP, 1944–1986 (Istoriko-statisticheski analiz).* Sofia: Institut po Istoriia na BKP pri TsK na BKP.

United States Agency for Global Media. 2018. *Audience and Impact: Overview for 2019.* Washington, DC: US Agency for Global Media.

United States Office of the Trade Representative. 2023. *National Trade Estimate Report on Foreign Non-Trade Barriers.* Washington, DC.

Uyghur Tribunal. 2021. *The Xinjiang Papers.* London: Uyghur Tribunal, https://shorturl.at/htJsO.

Vala, Carsten T. 2017. *The Politics of Protestant Churches and the Party-State in China: God Above Party?* New York: Routledge.

Van Slyke, Lyman P. 1967. *Enemies and Friends: The United Front in Chinese Communist History.* Stanford, CA: Stanford University Press.

Voice of America. 2021. "Qu 'niangpao' zan yanggang, Zhonggong de zhenshi yitu ke meiyou zhema jiandan." September 22.

Vortherms, Samantha A. 2024. *Manipulating Authoritarian Citizenship: Security, Development, and Local Membership in China*. Stanford, CA: Stanford University Press.

Walder, Andrew G. and Gong Xiaoxia. 1991. "Workers in the Tiananmen Protests." *The Australian Journal of Chinese Affairs* 29 (January): 1–29.

Wang Cijiang. 2013. *Chongtu yu zhili: Zhongguo quntixing shijian kaocha fenxi*. Beijing: Renmin Chubanshe.

Wang, Fei-Ling. 2005. *Organizing through Division and Exclusion: China's Hukou System*. Stanford, CA: Stanford University Press.

Wang, Huan and Ying Wang. 2023. "Party-Building and Government Funding: The Effect of the Chinese Communist Party on Non-Governmental Organizations." *Journal of Chinese Political Science* 28 (3): 427–447.

Wang, Jing. 2021. "'The Party Must Strengthen Its Leadership in Finance!': Digital Technologies and Financial Governance in China's Fintech Development." *The China Quarterly* 247: 773–792.

Wang Jingqing, ed. 2021. *Dang de jianshe yanjiu baogao 2021*. Beijing: Shehui Kexue Wenxian Chubanshe.

Wang Jingwen, Wang Fuqiu, Li Shuya, Wang Yinbo, and Qiu Zhaoyi. 2020. "Woguo bingxue yundong wenhua zijue de lujing yanjiu." *Shenyang Tiyu Xueyuan Xuebao* 39 (5): 138–144.

Wang, Peng and Xia Yan. 2020. "Bureaucratic Slack in China: The Anti-Corruption Campaign and the Decline of Patronage Networks in Developing Local Economies." *The China Quarterly* 243: 611–634.

Wang Xing. 2021. "Wenhua zijue shiyu xia de 'guochao' pinpai jueqi de chuanbo zhanlüe: Yi Zhongguo Lining weili." MA Thesis, School of Journalism and Communication, Northwest University.

Wang Yankun. 2009. "Guoxue re de chixu shengwen yu zhide sikao de jige wenti." *Jinan Xuebao* 31 (1): 138–145.

Wang, Yuhua and Carl Minzner. 2015. "The Rise of the Chinese Security State." *The China Quarterly* 222: 339–359.

Weber, Isabella. 2021. *How China Escaped Shock Therapy: The Market Reform Debate*. New York: Routledge.

Wedeman, Andrew. 2009. "Enemies of the State: Mass Incidents and Subversion in China." Paper presented at the Annual Meeting of the American Political Science Association, Toronto.

2012. *Double Paradox: Rapid Growth and Rising Corruption in China*. Ithaca, NY: Cornell University Press.

Weiss, Jessica Chen. 2014. *Powerful Patriots: Nationalist Protest in China's Foreign Relations*. New York: Oxford University Press.

Winters, Jeffrey A. 2011. *Oligarchy.* New York: Cambridge University Press.

Wong, Hayley. 2024. "Places of Worship Must 'Reflect Chinese Features.'" *South China Morning Post*, January 6, A8.

Xi Jinping. 2014. "Jianchi zongti guojia anquanguan zou Zhongguo tese guojia anquan daolu." www.xinhuanet.com//politics/2014 01/15/c_1110253910 .htm.

Xiang Zuotao. 2018. "Yuan Sudong diqu shehui zhuyi zhengdang de fazhan xianzhuang." *Zhonggong Zhongyang Dangxiao Xuebao* 22 (1): 60–68.

Xiao Jun and Chen Peng. 2022. "Guojia anquan shiye xia Haolaiwu dianying dui woguo wenhua anquan yingxiang de fansi: Jiyu 2012–2021 nian de yangben fenxi." *Dianying Wenxue*, no. 8: 21–27.

Xie Yungeng, ed. 2013. *Zhongguo shehui yuqing yu weiji guanli baogao 2013.* Beijing: Shehui Kexue Wenxian Chubanshe.

Xin, Ge and Jie Huang. 2022. "Party Building in an Unlikely Place? The Adaptive Presence of the Chinese Communist Party in the Non-Governmental Organizations (NGO)." *Journal of Contemporary China* 31 (135): 428–444.

Xin Zhongguo 50 nian tongji ziliao huibian. 1999. Beijing: Zhongguo Tongji Chubanshe.

Xinhua. 2004. *Xinhua zidian.* 10th ed. Beijing: Shangwu Yinshu Guan.

Xinjiang Weiwuer Zizhiqu Dangxiao. 1990. *Xiaoshi jishi 1950–1990.* Wulumuqi: Xinjiang Dangxiao Yinshuachang.

Xinjiang Weiwuer Zizhiqu Difangzhi Bianzuan Weiyuanhui. 2022. *Xinjiang tongzhi 1986–2005.* Beijing: Fangzhi Chubanshe.

Xizang Zizhiqu Difangzhi Bangongshi. 2021. *Xizang nianjian 2020.* Lasa: Xizang Renmin Chubanshe.

Xu, Jianhua and Siying He. 2022. "Can Grid Governance Fix the Party-State's Broken Windows? A Study of Stability Maintenance in Grassroots China." *The China Quarterly* 251: 843–865.

Xu, Yan. 2023. "Fragile Fortune: State Power and Concentrated Wealth in China." *Politics & Society* 51 (4): 597–624.

Xu Yihua et al. 2016. *Zongjiao yu Zhongguo guojia anquan yanjiu.* Beijing: Shishi Chubanshe.

Xue Xiaorong. 2018. *Hulianwang qiye dangjian: Jishu, ziben yu zhengzhi luoji zhangli xia de zhengdang zhili.* Beijing: Shishi Chubanshe.

Yan Daocheng. 2013. *Quntixing shijian zhong de wangluo yuqing yanjiu.* Beijing: Xinhua Chubanshe.

Yan, Xiaojun. 2014. "Engineering Stability: Authoritarian Political Control over University Students in Post-Deng China." *The China Quarterly* 218: 493–513.

Yan, Xiaojun and Jie Huang. 2017. "Navigating Unknown Waters: The Chinese Communist Party's New Presence in the Private Sector." *China Review* 17 (2): 37–63.

Yan, Xiaojun and Mohammed Alsudairi. 2021. "Guarding Against the Threat of a Westernizing Education: A Comparative Analysis of Chinese and Saudi Cultural Security Discourses and Practices Towards Overseas Study." *Journal of Contemporary China* 30 (131): 803–819.

Yang Shisheng and Zhang Yuxian. 2010. "Quanqiuhua xia de wenhua baquan yu wenhua anquan." *Qianyan*, no. 24: 160–162.

Yao Xiaoli and Wu Taigui. 2021. "Yunyong qukuailian jishu tuijin wangluo yishi xingtai anquan zhili: Jiazhi, tiaozhan yu duice." *Guangxi Keji Shifan Xueyuan Xuebao* 36 (6): 81–87.

Yu Zhonggui. 1990. *Fangjian baomi yu guojia anquan.* Beijing: Guofang Daxue Chubanshe.

Yun Shan. 2010. "Wenhua zijue, wenhua zixin, wenhua ziqiang." *Hongqi Wenzhai*, no. 15: 4–8, no. 16: 4–8, and no. 17: 4–9.

Zhang, Han and Jennifer Pan. 2019. "CASM: A Deep-Learning Approach for Collective-Action Events with Identifying Text and Image Data from Social Media." *Sociological Methodology* 49 (1): 1–57.

Zhang, Liang, comp. 2001. *The Tiananmen Papers.* New York: Public Affairs.

Zhang Mingjun and Chen Ming. 2014. "2013 niandu Zhongguo shehui dianxing quntixing shijian fenxi baogao." *Zhongguo Shehui Gonggong Anquan Yanjiu Baogao*, no. 5: 3–12.

Zhang Xiaoping. 2012. *Dangqian Zhongguo wenhua anquan wenti yanjiu.* Beijing: Shehui Kexue Wenxian Chubanshe.

Zhang, Zhu. 2021. "Wealth Without Power: The Rise of China's Super-Rich and Their Relationship with the Communist Party." PhD Dissertation, Department of Political Science, Tulane University.

Zhao Yingchen. 2004. "Quanqiuhua beijing xia de Zhongguo wenhua anquan." *Lanzhou Xuekan*, no. 6: 36–38.

Zhejiang Gong'an Shizhi Bianzuan Weiyuanhui. 2021. *Zhejiang gong'an nianjian 2020.* Hangzhou: Zhejiang Renmin Chubanshe.

Zhonggong Zhongyang Bangongting and Guowuyuan Bangongting. 2014. *Guanyu chuangxin qunzhong gongzuo fangfa jiejue xinfang tuchu wenti de yijian.* February 25.

Zhonggong Zhongyang Guojia Jiguan Gongzuo Weiyuanhui Yanjiushi. 2008. *Zhonggong zhongyang guojia jiguan gongzuo baogao 2008.* Beijing: Zhonggong Zhongyang Guojia Jiguan Gongzuo Weiyuanhui Yanjiushi.

Zhonggong Zhongyang Zuzhi Bu. 2002. *Zhongguo gongchandang dangnei tongji ziliao huibian, 1921–2000*. Beijing: Zhonggong Zhongyang Zuzhi Bu Xinxi Guanli Zhongxin.

——. 2011. *Zhongguo gongchandang dangnei tongji ziliao huibian, 1921–2010*. Beijing: Dangjian Duwu Chubanshe.

——. 2013. "Dangyuan 8512.7 wan ming, jiceng dangzu 420.1 wan ge, dangyuan duiwu he jiceng dang zuzhi pengbo shengji he huoli." Beijing: Zhonggong Zhongyang Zuzhi Bu.

——. 2014. "2013 nian Zhongguo gongchandang dangnei tongji gongbao." Beijing: Zhonggong Zhongyang Zuzhi Bu.

——. 2015. "2014 nian Zhongguo gongchandang dangnei tongji gongbao." Beijing: Zhonggong Zhongyang Zuzhi Bu.

——. 2016. "2015 nian Zhongguo gongchandang dangnei tongji gongbao." Beijing: Zhonggong Zhongyang Zuzhi Bu.

——. 2017. "2016 nian Zhongguo gongchandang dangnei tongji gongbao." Beijing: Zhonggong Zhongyang Zuzhi Bu.

——. 2018. "2017 nian Zhongguo gongchandang dangnei tongji gongbao." Beijing: Zhonggong Zhongyang Zuzhi Bu.

——. 2019. "2018 nian Zhongguo gongchandang dangnei tongji gongbao." Beijing: Zhonggong Zhongyang Zuzhi Bu.

——. 2020. "2019 nian Zhongguo gongchandang dangnei tongji gongbao." Beijing: Zhonggong Zhongyang Zuzhi Bu.

——. 2021a. "Zhongguo gongchandang dangnei tongji gongbao." Beijing: Zhonggong Zhongyang Zuzhi Bu.

——. 2021b. *Zhongguo gongchandang zuzhi jianshe 100 nian*. Beijing: Dangjian Duwu Chubanshe.

——. 2022. "2021 nian Zhongguo gongchandang dangnei tongji gongbao." Beijing: Zhonggong Zhongyang Zuzhi Bu.

——. 2023. "Zhongguo gongchandang dangnei tongji gongbao." Beijing: Zhonggong Zhongyang Zuzhi Bu.

——. 2024. "Zhongguo gongchandang dangnei tongji gongbao." Beijing: Zhonggong Zhongyang Zuzhi Bu.

Zhongguo tongji nianjian. 2010. Beijing: Zhongguo Tongji Chubanshe.

——. 2018. Beijing: Zhongguo Tongji Chubanshe.

——. 2023. Beijing: Zhongguo Tongji Chubanshe.

Zhongyang Zhengfawei Bangongting. 2021a. *Ping'an Zhongguo nianjian 2019*. Beijing: Zhongguo Chang'an Chuban Chuanmei Youxian Gongsi.

——. 2021b. *Ping'an Zhongguo nianjian 2020*. Beijing: Zhongguo Chang'an Chuban Chuanmei Youxian Gongsi.

Zhou, Kai. 2018. "A New Model of Control? Party Penetration of Civil Society Organizations in Contemporary China." Harvard-Yenching Institute Working Paper Series.

Zhu Xiaoming. 2005. "Lun 'Zhongguo tese shehui zhuyi zongjiao guan': Guanyu xin shiqi zongjiao gongzuo shijian fazhan he lilun chuangxin de sikao." *Zhongyang Shehui Zhuyi Xueyuan Xuekan*, no. 1: 5–17.

Zongti Guojia Anquan Guan Ganbu Duben Bianweihui. 2016. *Zongti Guojia Anquan Guan Ganbu Duben*. Beijing: Renmin Chubanshe.

Zuo Fengrong. 2022. "Zhongguo xuejie Sulian jubian wenti yanjiu shi huimou." *Dangdai Shijie Shehui Zhuyi Wenti*, no. 2: 38–45.

Acknowledgments

In writing this Element, I have incurred debts to individuals and institutions that I am happy to acknowledge in the lines below. I am grateful to audiences that provided feedback during talks at the Aleksanteri Institute (Finland); at the Institute for International and European Affairs (Dublin); at the Taipei School of Economics and Political Science (twice); at Southern Methodist University; at the Chinese University of Hong Kong (Shenzhen); at Zhejiang University; at Bard College (Berlin); at the Virtual Workshop on Chinese Politics; at the Annual Meeting of the Association for Asian Studies (twice); and at the Annual Meeting of the American Political Science Association. I am also grateful to Hiroki Takeuchi, Saul Wilson, Austin Jordan, and Ma Ming for helpful conversations. The three co-editors of the series Elements in Politics and Society in East Asia (Erin Aeran Chung, Mary Alice Haddad, and Benjamin L. Read) provided invaluable advice, steady encouragement, and constructive feedback. I also want to thank the anonymous reviewer for Cambridge University Press, who offered thoughtful suggestions for revisions. As usual, this study benefited from the care and attention of Nancy Hearst. At Tulane, the School of Liberal Arts and the Office of Academic Affairs provided much appreciated grants, and Jiachen Shi and Yipeng Zhang offered research assistance. I wrote this Element with my students in mind. It would not have been possible without my teachers. Among these, Jean Oi stands out for her kindness and exemplary commitment to her students. I dedicate this book to her.

Cambridge Elements ⁼

Politics and Society in East Asia

Erin Aeran Chung
The Johns Hopkins University

Erin Aeran Chung is the Charles D. Miller Professor of East Asian Politics in the Department of Political Science at the Johns Hopkins University. She specializes in East Asian political economy, migration and citizenship, and comparative racial politics. She is the author of *Immigration and Citizenship in Japan* (Cambridge, 2010, 2014; Japanese translation, Akashi Shoten, 2012) and *Immigrant Incorporation in East Asian Democracies* (Cambridge, 2020). Her research has been supported by grants from the Academy of Korean Studies, the Japan Foundation, the Japan Foundation Center for Global Partnership, the Social Science Research Council, and the American Council of Learned Societies.

Mary Alice Haddad
Wesleyan University

Mary Alice Haddad is the John E. Andrus Professor of Government, East Asian Studies, and Environmental Studies at Wesleyan University. Her research focuses on democracy, civil society, and environmental politics in East Asia as well as city diplomacy around the globe. A Fulbright and Harvard Academy scholar, Haddad is author of *Effective Advocacy: Lessons from East Asia's Environmentalists* (MIT, 2021), *Building Democracy in Japan* (Cambridge, 2012), and *Politics and Volunteering in Japan* (Cambridge, 2007), and co-editor of *Greening East Asia* (University of Washington, 2021), and *NIMBY is Beautiful* (Berghahn Books, 2015). She has published in journals such as *Comparative Political Studies*, *Democratization*, *Journal of Asian Studies*, and *Nonprofit and Voluntary Sector Quarterly*, with writing for the public appearing in the *Asahi Shimbun*, the *Hartford Courant*, and the *South China Morning Post*.

Benjamin L. Read
University of California, Santa Cruz

Benjamin L. Read is a professor of Politics at the University of California, Santa Cruz. His research has focused on local politics in China and Taiwan, and he also writes about issues and techniques in comparison and field research. He is author of *Roots of the State: Neighborhood Organization and Social Networks in Beijing and Taipei* (Stanford, 2012), coauthor of *Field Research in Political Science: Practices and Principles* (Cambridge, 2015), and co-editor of *Local Organizations and Urban Governance in East and Southeast Asia: Straddling State and Society* (Routledge, 2009). His work has appeared in journals such as *Comparative Political Studies*, *Comparative Politics*, the *Journal of Conflict Resolution*, the *China Journal*, the *China Quarterly*, and *the Washington Quarterly*, as well as several edited books.

About the Series

The Cambridge Elements series on Politics and Society in East Asia offers original, multidisciplinary contributions on enduring and emerging issues in the dynamic region of East Asia by leading scholars in the field. Suitable for general readers and specialists alike, these short, peer-reviewed volumes examine common challenges and patterns within the region while identifying key differences between countries. The series consists of two types of contributions: 1) authoritative field surveys of established concepts and themes that offer roadmaps for further research; and 2) new research on emerging issues that challenge conventional understandings of East Asian politics and society. Whether focusing on an individual country or spanning the region, the contributions in this series connect regional trends with points of theoretical debate in the social sciences and will stimulate productive interchanges among students, researchers, and practitioners alike.

Cambridge Elements ⁼

Politics and Society in East Asia

Elements in the Series

The East Asian Covid-19 Paradox
Yves Tiberghien

State, Society, and Markets in North Korea
Andrew Yeo

The Digital Transformation and Japan's Political Economy
Ulrike Schaede and Kay Shimizu

Japan as a Global Military Power: New Capabilities, Alliance Integration, Bilateralism-Plus
Christopher W. Hughes

State and Social Protests in China
Yongshun Cai and Chih-Jou Jay Chen

The State and Capitalism in China
Margaret Pearson, Meg Rithmire, and Kellee Tsai

Political Selection in China: Rethinking Foundations and Findings
Melanie Manion

Environmental Politics in East Asia
Mary Alice Haddad

Politics of the North Korean Diaspora
Sheena Chestnut Greitens

The Adaptability of the Chinese Communist Party
Martin K. Dimitrov

A full series listing is available at: www.cambridge.org/EPEA

Printed in the United States
by Baker & Taylor Publisher Services